Getting to *Why*

A Practical Guide to Finding Your Highest Purpose

by

JB SYMONS, PhD

with

Matt Rouge, MSM

Getting to *Why*
A Practical Guide to Finding Your Highest Purpose

by JB Symons, PhD
with Matt Rouge, MSM

Illustrations by Alexandra Douglass
Book design by Cheryl Perez
Workbook design by Andrew Norris

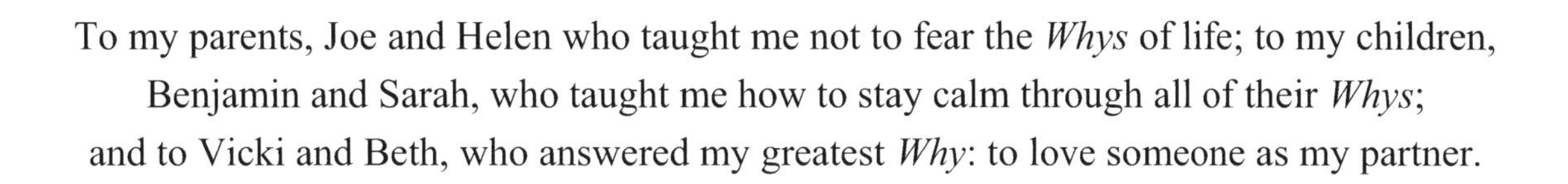

To my parents, Joe and Helen who taught me not to fear the *Whys* of life; to my children,
Benjamin and Sarah, who taught me how to stay calm through all of their *Whys*;
and to Vicki and Beth, who answered my greatest *Why*: to love someone as my partner.

JB Symons

To my daughter Eleanor. May your life be filled with amazing *Whys!*

Matt Rouge

CONTENTS

Introduction

Congratulations! You are ready for a complete and positive transformation of your life. Before we begin, let me tell you *Why* I decided to write this book, the first in the *Getting To* series.

For over 40 years, I have been teaching, learning from, observing, praying for, coaching, preaching to, and mentoring thousands of individuals in all walks of life. I have worked with the C-level executives, mid-level managers, and worker bees of over 300 companies and organizations, celebrating with them when they succeeded and crying with them when they failed. I have worked with some of the most mentally, emotionally, socially, and spiritually developed people on the planet, as well as some at the other end of the spectrum. All of the stories you read in this book are true and come from my experiences.

People almost always have had the same response when I asked them my number one consulting question: *Why?*

"*Why* are you living the way you're living?"

"*Why* do you have the job you have?"

"*Why* do you associate with your current group of friends?"

"*Why* are you doing things this way in your company?"

The usual response? "That's a good question. I need to give that some thought."

I've written this book to help them—and you—get to *Why*. The keystone in the arch of the *Getting To* series, this book will help you find your higher purpose in life, allowing you to be more happy and effective in everything you do. Turn the page and start *Getting to Why!*

PART ONE

UNDERSTANDING WHY

Chapter One

Why *Why?*

Why is *the* mission question—the biggest and most important in your life. *Why* is not a complaint or a challenge to an argument; rather, it is a perception, a paradigm of high magnitude. *Why* begins deep within you, pushing and pulling you into the unknown, to the boundaries of your current understanding. *Why* is the beginning of consequential thinking.

Why can be physical, as when you look out at the stars and ponder *Why* the universe has taken the form it has.

Why can be mental, as when you wonder *Why* a particular mathematical proof is true.

Why can be emotional, as when you wonder *Why* you have fallen in love or out of love with someone.

Why can be spiritual, as when you ponder *Why* you exist.

Why seeks to define itself physically, mentally, emotionally, and spiritually in multiple forms because it desires an end point or at least a horizon. *Why* is purpose itself.

It's time to check the compass of your life.

Why is the fifth point on the compass of your life; it's the dot on the map that says, "You are here." With it come 360 degrees of options. *Why* is the mantra of the pioneer because courage and initiative appear when you ask it, preparing you for the *Who*, *What*, *Which*, *When*, *Where*, *How*, and *If* of your journeys. Without *Why*, however, you are just a wanderer among life's many choices.

Why is the first question you asked as a child. Like many of us, you may have received a poor, incomplete, or defensive response: "Because I told you so," or, "Don't ask questions—just do it!" (This was your first introduction to the poor management and supervisory techniques you have experienced in your life and may even use yourself.) These *Whys* of your early life were not only *Whys* of curiosity but were also *Whys* of passion. You *really* wanted to know *Why!*

Why is the fifth point on the compass
of your life.

GETTING TO
WHY

The way you asked *Why* and handled the responses in your early childhood established your pattern of development and ultimately your path in life. You may have continued to ask questions and seek answers boldly regardless of negative feedback. You may have accepted a more cautious approach while continuing to ask and explore. Or you may have accepted the *don't ask, just do it* response and faced life with your head down, looking up only when you ran into something.

You deserve to ask *Why!*

All human beings desire and deserve to struggle with the *Whys* of their lives. A child may ask, "*Why* is the sky blue?" A philosopher may ask, "*Why* are we here?" An employee may ask, "*Why* are we doing this, and *Why* are we doing it this way?" Everyone really wants to know *Why*.

In your heart, so do you. Can you accept that the right to ask *Why* is not something that you need to earn or can ever have taken from you? Whether you are in prison or a ten million dollar home, the question is yours to ask, and you were born with permission to do so.

I believe that the Higher Power desires us to ask *Why* and gives us permission to do so at any time in our lives: "Ask, and it shall be given you; seek, and ye shall find; knock, and it shall be opened unto you" (Matthew 7:7, King James Version).

The Chinese classic *Dao De Jing* begins (as translated by Matt), "The way that can be said to be the way is not the invariable way. The name that can be said to be the name is not the invariable name." Similarly, *Why* may seem bigger than your ability to define it, and it may be frustrating at times to see and feel the end you seek. I promise you, however, that the journey is worth all the effort you will exert. You deserve your *Whys*—all of them.

The paradox of *Why* is that the starting point and ending point are the same: once you ask *Why*, you're there. Yet *Why* is not a question to be asked once, but rather again and again. Your answers to *Why* will transform themselves as time passes, as circumstances change, and as you gain in knowledge and wisdom; and your destinations and experiences will become richer and deeper.

Working with *Why* leads you to your own highest purpose. Working against *Why* invariably puts you in a rut. To extend and transform the metaphor, a rut is a grave with both ends kicked out. If you don't feel fulfilled in life, if you feel as though you're barely alive to begin with, then what's the risk in asking *Why?*

Why is you, *Why* is greater than you, and *Why* invites you to be greater than the current you. When you get to *Why*, your chances of achieving success, fulfillment, and peace increase dramatically. If you don't get to *Why*—all bets are off.

Some questions to ponder.

If you're ready, ask yourself the following: *Why* are you doing what you do today? *Why* are you associating with the people in your life? *Why* are you going in the direction you're going?

Can you answer these questions with emotion and passion? If you cannot, you'll have the first of many chances to ask yourself *Why* in the following pages. If you can, you'll have the chance to enrich and move even deeper into your answers.

Although in this book you are encouraged to ask *Why* to discover your highest purpose, you can and should apply *Why* to less weighty matters as well. In fact, in tackling any problem or pursuing any opportunity, *Why* is the first question to ask.

The good news is that it's possible to get to *Why* at any time in your life. It's also possible to leave *Why* along the way and get back to it. This book provides concepts, examples, and tools to help you get to *Why*, whether for the first time or after a departure from it. Remember, you are never too young or too old to ask *Why!*

Please perform the exercise for this chapter in the workbook at the back of this book. The entire workbook may also be downloaded in PDF format for free at www.gettingtowhy.com.

Chapter Two

Pleasure and Satisfaction

In order to get to *Why*, you need to have a vision of what your emotional state will be like after you arrive. After all, you're not asking yourself *Why* in order to feel worse, are you?

Most normal people want to live their lives in a state of happiness but do not understand that happiness has two components: pleasure and satisfaction. Contrariwise, unhappiness also has two components: pain and dissatisfaction. The following graph shows the relationship of these elements to each other.

The Four Quadrants of Fulfillment

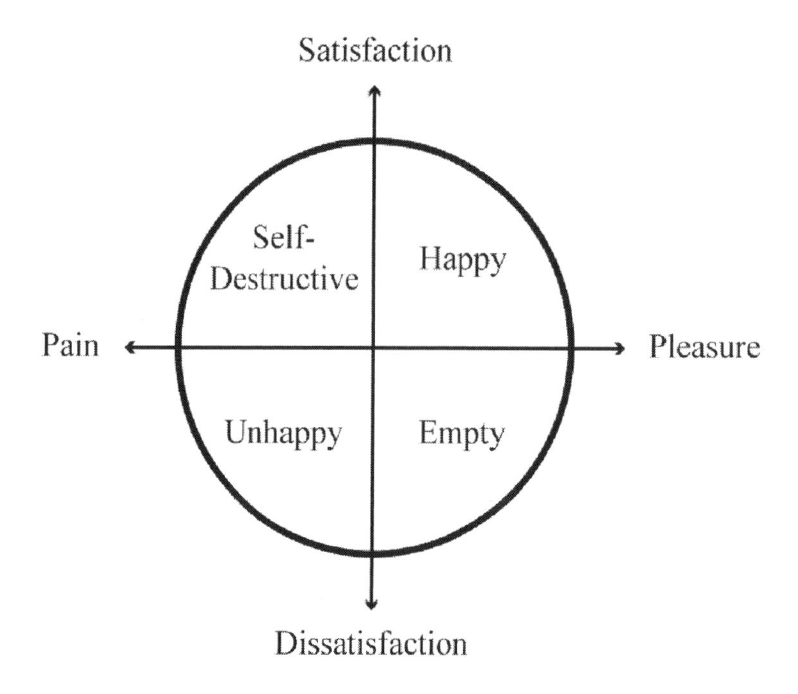

The x-axis is the classic pleasure-pain spectrum found in every psychological discipline. The y-axis adds a new distinction, the satisfaction-dissatisfaction spectrum. What's the difference between the two?

Pleasure *and* satisfaction—both are essential to happiness.

Pleasure and pain are aspects of our sensations, whether physical or emotional, and we can experience a jumble of both at the same time. For example, we can be in love yet have a toothache. We can be fearful about our finances yet hopeful about a new sales prospect. We can be enjoying a meal yet beginning to feel full and uncomfortable. The aggregate of our pain and pleasure can be a bit difficult to assess, but we can imagine what total pleasure would be like: health, wealth, great friends, good food, adventures, peace and quiet, or whatever we happen to desire.

In contrast, satisfaction and dissatisfaction arise from our judgment of a particular situation or of our life as a whole. For example, you may be getting pleasure from a delicious meal yet feel dissatisfied with it because of its small portions or high price. You may be receiving painful sensations from a shot in the arm yet be satisfied with the situation because you know the immunization will protect you from influenza. You may be receiving great pleasure overall in your life yet feel dissatisfied because you feel you are not reaching your potential. Or perhaps you have reached it yet nevertheless feel dissatisfied because you are envious of a friend who is doing better.

In short, pain and pleasure are absolute; satisfaction and dissatisfaction are relative.

Satisfaction and dissatisfaction are extremely important when it comes to assessing how you are doing in your Seven Areas of Life (which we will introduce in the following two chapters). Your boss may be demanding at times, but are you satisfied with your career? Your spouse may cook wonderful dinners, but are you dissatisfied with your home life? When it comes to life as a whole, you feel satisfaction or its opposite deep in your being.

The pleasure-pain axis and the satisfaction-dissatisfaction axis form four quadrants, each of which corresponds to a distinct emotional state. I call this graph the "Four Quadrants of Fulfillment," since the quadrants relate to our ultimate goal of happiness, or fulfillment. We can assess our life as a whole, or we can look at each of the Seven Areas individually.

Happy (pleasure + satisfaction). This is where we all want to be. We are enjoying all the pleasures of life, and we are deeply satisfied with our Seven Areas of Life and life as a whole. The person in this quadrant has asked and answered *Why*. Another appropriate name for this quadrant is "Fulfilled," or "Joyful."

Empty (pleasure + dissatisfaction). This is a conflicted quadrant in which the person is experiencing pleasure without meaning. He or she most likely has failed to ask *Why* and has instead simply aimed to acquire what society says are the good things in life. Lacking his or her own goals and standards of success in the Seven Areas of Life, this person finds satisfaction hard to grasp.

Unhappy (pain + dissatisfaction). Most of us have found ourselves in this position at one time or another. There are lots of things going on that we don't like, and the result dissatisfies us. Another appropriate name for this quadrant is "Unfulfilled."

Self-Destructive (pain + satisfaction). This is the second of the conflicted quadrants, and there are several different reasons *Why* people may find themselves here. There may be so much self-hatred or self-anger that a person is satisfied to be in pain. Another person may find perverse satisfaction in addictions and cycles of hitting rock bottom and then recovering. (A special case is someone who is suffering from an illness or some other great source of pain who nevertheless is leading a satisfying life. Such a person would obviously not be self-destructive. In this quadrant we are referring to people who actually take satisfaction in their own pain.)

Are you living in the dead center of life?

Most of us tend to live our lives in the dead center of the graph above, or perhaps slightly within the **Unhappy** quadrant:

The Four Quadrants of Fulfillment

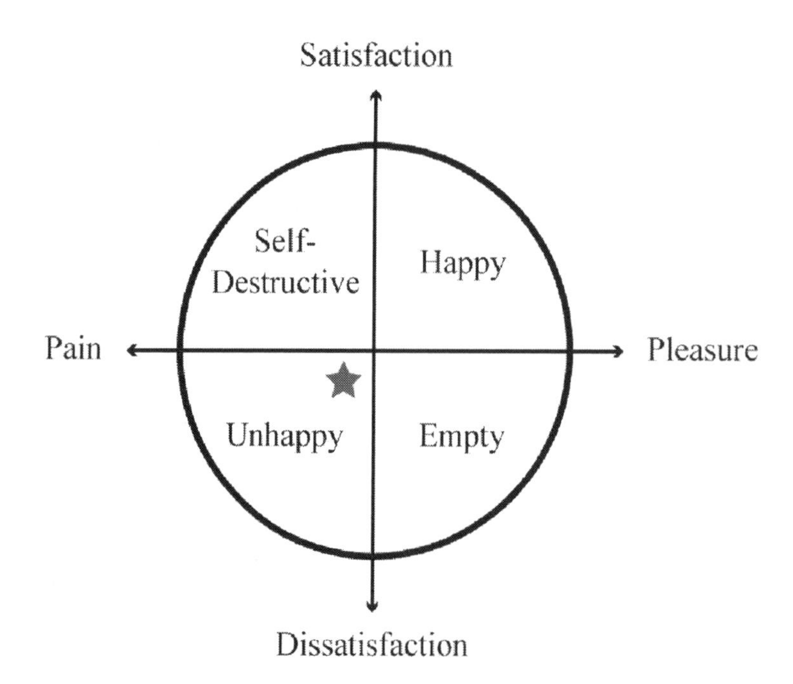

In this situation, we're experiencing neither great pain nor great pleasure in our lives. If we are struggling to ask ourselves *Why*, we may not know how to assess whether we are satisfied with things or not. This is one of the truly great pitfalls of life. In this insipid, uninspired state, we too often think that eliminating a bit more pain and achieving a bit more pleasure will at last get us to where we want to be. Yet the Happy quadrant will elude us if we do not ask *Why*.

The story of Bill (achieving pleasure and satisfaction).

The story of Bill illustrates how getting to *Why* can be the key to obtaining that combination of pleasure and satisfaction called "happiness" or "fulfillment."

Bill was the president of a small architectural engineering company that specialized in designing churches, schools, and a variety of public buildings. In addition to his duties as CEO, Bill was the chief architect of the company. His father had also been an architect and the company's founder. More than anything else, Bill valued his father's legacy and was determined to maintain the company as a going concern.

Bill was very dissatisfied with his two salespersons, who, being engineers, were as good at engineering as they were bad at presenting and closing sales. As a result of their lack of competence in this area, revenue growth in the firm had completely stalled. Not wanting to lay off any employees, Bill was experiencing pain—pain that came from financing the company with personal loans that he could ill afford.

Bill called on me to help him get out of this rut. I performed a SWOT analysis (Strengths, Weaknesses, Opportunities, Threats) of the company, inviting all 26 employees to participate. I also attended a sales presentation by the two engineers, as well as one by Bill. Immediately, I noticed three things:

Bill felt he couldn't go out and sell because he had to run the company.
Bill was by far the best salesman of the company.
Bill didn't know who could run the company if he were outside selling.

After we reviewed the SWOT analysis, I asked the four senior leaders of the company to fill out five job descriptions: one each for the president, himself, and his three colleagues. I wanted to see how detailed and frank their job descriptions would be, especially concerning their own positions. I received their descriptions, read them thoroughly, and then sat down with Bill to review them.

"Bill," I said, "you yourself need to go out and sell because you have non-salespersons in sales positions. You know more about this company, have more passion about this company, and communicate that passion better than anyone else here. I don't want you in this office more than two days a week. Less than that is preferable. You enjoy selling, right?"

"Yes, I love it," said Bill, aghast, "but who would run the business?"

I showed him the job description for president that one of his vice presidents had written; it was five pages long and full of perceptive detail.

"Bill," I said, "this man just applied for the position."

Bill became CEO and the company's sole salesperson.

GETTING TO WHY

"But he's one of my best engineers," said Bill.

"Even better," I said. "He'll have high expectations."

Bill implemented my suggestion of a 60-day trial period in which the vice president became president and Bill became CEO and the company's sole salesperson. The results astonished even me: during the period, Bill closed three sales worth more than $5 million, enough business to sustain the company for another 18 months. Within one year, the company had doubled in size and was averaging almost $30 million in revenue per year.

Leveraging this success, Bill adopted a new goal of working just three days a week, which he accomplished in his second year of selling. A few years later, Bill sold his business to a buyer that promised to retain all of the company's employees, and he was able to retire a multimillionaire at age 52. He has now been traveling and teaching leadership for five years. In a relatively short period of time, he went from dissatisfaction with his career to tremendous satisfaction, from the pain of poor sales and money troubles to the tremendous pleasure of doing what he loves. Bill is living in the upper right quadrant. He's happy.

Please perform the exercise for this chapter in the workbook at the back of this book. The entire workbook may also be downloaded in PDF format for free at www.gettingtowhy.com.

CHAPTER THREE

SUCCESS AND FAILURE

What we learned in the previous chapter allows us to define success: living in the upper right **Happy** quadrant, where we experience both pleasure and satisfaction. (Needless to say, true success comes only when we achieve pleasure and satisfaction through moral and ethical means.)

Most people in the **Happy** quadrant have arrived there first by understanding *Why* and then achieving *Why*. Only a small percentage will ever stumble into happiness without first getting to *Why*. As I said in the first chapter, *Why* is fifth point on the compass of life: it lets you know where you are in the four quadrants and take action to move to a new and better place.

In contrast, the other three quadrants represent forms of failure. People in the **Self-Destructive** quadrant are acting irrationally and may not be interested in or capable of getting to *Why* in the first place. People in the **Unhappy** quadrant either have not yet gotten to *Why* and may be struggling to ask the question. People in the **Empty** quadrant best illustrate the importance of getting to *Why*, since the pleasure they are experiencing is completely mismatched with the *Why* they have yet to grasp.

Understand your own standard of success.

Failure is real; failure can be a matter of life and death. In Vietnam, too many times I saw failure result in the deaths of beloved friends standing right next to me. In my work as a pastor and later a business consultant, despite my best efforts and fervent prayers, I have seen businesses and organizations crumble before my eyes due to a failure of leadership. I have seen marriages go down the drain. I have seen people lose everything even when the solutions to their problems were obvious and understood and accepted by them.

But success is also real, and I have seen many an individual and many a company step back from the brink of destruction and move dramatically toward the **Happy** quadrant, which is success itself.

More often than not, this attainment of success was the direct result of people getting to *Why*, then realizing their *Why* through *Who*, *What*, *Which*, *When*, *Where*, *How*, and *If*.

Just as each and everyone's *Why* is different, so is everyone's standard of success. If you are in prison and suffer from addictions, your first step to success is overcoming these problems. If you live in a $10 million home, you might decide that success for you means buying an even more spectacular home. Or you might decide that success means selling everything and focusing on charitable causes. Asking *Why* reveals a multitude of options.

Today's success is not necessarily tomorrow's. A person might overcome addictions one day but succumb again to them a year later. A person might make a killing in the stock market but lose it all at a subsequent date. Similarly, a person might be in a marriage or job that seems rocky at first but turns out to be the relationship or calling of a lifetime.

It is essential to add a word of warning here. There is a temptation to look at what people have achieved in life and judge their success or lack of it by our own standards. Talking with them, however, may well reveal that they are absolutely content and at peace. Don't let your own measuring system blind you to others' pleasure and satisfaction. We shouldn't attempt to set the bar for others, nor should we allow them to do so for us.

What we can do for each other, however, is ask *Why*. Instead of asking a judgmental question, we can ask the *Why* question. For example, "You say you're happy with where you are in life. *Why* is that?" But be prepared to answer the same question when people take a look at your life.

The true stories that follow illustrate how people can be successes or failures in asking and answering *Why*.

The story of Kelly (finding success).

Thirty years old, brilliant, and acknowledged by others for her creativity and high energy level, Kelly was unhappy but couldn't say *Why*. She had worked in sales at a five-star hotel for six months and was very good at her job. Then again, she had always done well at everything she had attempted to do.

I asked her to complete a profile assessment that gave me information about her thought processes, personality, and areas of professional interest. I then asked her to tell me about the jobs that she had held and rate each from 1 to 10 as to the pleasure and satisfaction they had brought her. Of the nine jobs that she had held since college, one stuck out: she had given the highest ratings possible to her job as production coordinator for a local civic theater.

"*Why* aren't you still doing that?" I asked.

"Oh, a couple reasons," said Kelly. "It didn't pay well. I had to work another job at the same time just to survive. And the production director was very hard to work with."

"*Why* don't you become a production director?" I asked. "You experienced a 10 out of 10 in both pleasure and satisfaction at this job. That's pretty rare."

"I would love to," said Kelly, "but where are the opportunities?"

I thought for a moment, then said, "Three questions come to mind. Have you looked in the major theater publications for a job?"

"No," said Kelly.

"Have you looked at local civic theaters?" I asked.

"No," said Kelly.

"What about the company you work for?" I asked. "You guys own eight four- and five-star facilities. Don't these resorts put on major productions and need someone to coordinate all the seating, lighting—all that kind of stuff?"

Kelly's eyes lit up. "That's a great idea!" she said. "I could talk to the CEO about bringing in plays and productions and coordinating everything. I'd never thought of that before!"

As of this writing, Kelly's company is considering her idea. Even if her dream job does not materialize at her current company, her getting to *Why* and establishing her personal standard of success has empowered her to seek her dream position or convince a company to create it for her.

The next true story is not so pleasant.

The story of Vince and Mary.

A young couple, whom we'll call Vince and Mary, came to me and asked me to perform their wedding ceremony. She was working on her master of arts in education and was teaching at a local school. He was working on a tough, three-year combination MBA-JD program. Both were doing very well in school.

Before I will marry a couple, I require them to go through a minimum of three counseling sessions, and I permit absolutely no exceptions. I always administer a battery of personality and behavioral assessments, since people in love lose all objectivity, and the process helps them achieve a better understanding of their future partner and themselves.

The number one job of a counselor in this situation is to ask a lot of *Whys*. *Why* do you love this person? *Why* do you think you'll be good together over the long term? *Why* did you choose him or her and not someone else? The answers, or the lack thereof, can be surprising.

Despite my desire to see both of these young people in the best light possible, by the second session I could do nothing to avoid the opinion that Vince was one of the most arrogant, condescending, and controlling persons I had ever met. I was also disturbed by the fact that Mary was visibly hurt by this behavior without doing anything to push back.

I asked if I could meet with them independently, and they agreed. During my session with Mary, I learned that Vince was also verbally abusive. To make matters worse, Mary seemed quite fearful of providing frank and honest answers to my various *Why* questions about the relationship. I grew increasingly concerned.

During my session with Vince, I learned that he was an only child and had always received his heart's desire from doting, wealthy parents so long as he got all A's on his report card, a requirement he had never failed to fulfill. When I asked Vince to give me one example of a time he had shared something with someone, he drew a blank. My concern now morphed into dread.

The next time the three of us got together, I said, "There are only three names that go at the bottom of the marriage license—yours and mine, and I take this responsibility very seriously. I'd like you to consider postponing the marriage until you know each other better and have better skills in communicating, cooperating, understanding, and trusting."

Hearing this, Vince flew into a rage. "You think we're going to postpone this because of what *you* think? You've got to be joking!"

Vince stormed out of the room, dragging a dejected Mary with him.

GETTING TO WHY

"No sir," I said, looking him in the eye and speaking in a calm voice. "You two have no idea *Why* you are marrying each other. And you, Vince, have some issues to sort out before you're ready for this big step."

What Vince then said cannot be repeated in this book. He stormed out of the room, dragging a dejected Mary with him. They proceeded to get married on the date originally planned, and Mary asked for an annulment a mere 29 days later. She also returned to my office for counseling for the next six months. Vince's verbal abuse had immediately turned into physical abuse, and his inability to share had been exposed in a manner that Mary had been unable to tolerate.

Vince and Mary had personal *Whys* that were incompatible with each other's potential happiness. His *Why*, which he could neither face nor admit, consisted of obtaining a beautiful, smart, obedient, malleable, and non-confrontational wife (notice I did not say "partner"). Mary was just another A on his report card.

Mary's *Why*, likewise hidden to her, consisted of obtaining a handsome, brilliant, high-achieving, and powerful man. Mary saw too late that his desire to achieve power came at any cost, including her dignity, self-respect, and safety. Vince would never have been concerned about her reaching the **Happy** quadrant; he cared only about himself.

In truly great relationships, personal or professional, the participants are interested in helping each other get to that upper right quadrant, the zone of happiness and true success. If you do not feel that the people who are important to you hope for your success, you need to consider *Why* that is. And you should likewise ask yourself whether you have the same kind of hope for your friends and loved ones.

Please perform the exercise for this chapter in the workbook at the back of this book. The entire workbook may also be downloaded in PDF format for free at www.gettingtowhy.com.

CHAPTER FOUR

THE SEVEN AREAS OF LIFE

The concept of there being distinct areas of life has been popular in psychological circles for decades (with the ultimate originator unclear). It's a powerful concept, and my version that follows has helped thousands of people divide their lives into easy-to-grasp components for better management of the parts and the whole.

The Seven Areas of Life

In this graphic, life is a circle with the areas forming sections of equal size around the core of Self. Further, all of the areas touch each other and influence each other. (You will notice the resemblance of this graphic to the Eight Words graphic at the end of this book.)

It is important not to get trapped in any one of the roles we play. If we do so, as the graphic suggests, our Self will be off-center, and the wheel will no longer roll smoothly. Rather, it is essential that we establish the proper balance among the roles so as to honor the core of Self. We can achieve this balance only by getting to *Why* in each of the seven areas, just as we must in our life as a whole.

The following is an overview of each of the Seven Areas of Life:

Physical and Health
Your physical wellness and fitness, as well as everything you do to maintain and improve your body: diet, exercise, yoga, Pilates, etc.

Mental and Educational
Your mental wellness and attainments, as well as everything you do to maintain and improve your mental state: classes, seminars, training, reading, journaling, therapy, etc.

Spiritual
Your relationship with God or what you perceive as Divine, as well as everything you do to maintain and build that relationship: attending religious ceremonies, prayer, meditation, etc.

Social
Your relationships with your friends and society as a whole, as well as everything you do to maintain these relationships: spending time with people, playing sports, belonging to clubs and organizations, joining causes, etc.

Family and Home
Your relationships with your family members and your life at home, including all of the practices and traditions that sustain and enhance a harmonious coexistence: fun family activities, meals together, family religious practices and events, holiday get-togethers and reunions, etc. This area also includes finding a life partner and maintaining a relationship with him or her.

Financial
Your relationship with money, including cash flow from work and investments, cash outflow from purchases of necessities and luxuries, debt management, etc.

Career
Your relationship with your work or, in other words, the activities you perform to add value to the world, including development of skills and knowledge, advancing to higher positions, making transitions to fulfill long-term goals, etc. Not just your "job."

The Areas of Life are interrelated.

Clearly, each of the areas influences and overlaps with the others. For example, your family life will have a very direct connection with your social life, and most (but not all) people will use their career to provide money for their financial life. Having good mental health and a suitable education is essential to a solid career, and so on.

As elaborated in a previous chapter, you can evaluate your life as a whole in terms of pleasure and satisfaction and place yourself in one of the Quadrants of Fulfillment. It is also advisable to evaluate each of your areas of life independently and place yourself on a separate Quadrants of Fulfillment graph for each. For example, a person may find that he or she has a **Happy** family life, an **Empty** mental life, an **Unhappy** physical life, and a **Self-Destructive** career—all at the same time.

Why should you take care to evaluate all seven areas? It is possible to find yourself outside the **Happy** quadrant for your life as a whole yet not understand the reason *Why* you are not there. Paying careful attention to each of the areas will usually provide you with better clarity about your life in its entirety.

When someone comes to me for help in one area of life, more often than not we end up discovering that other areas require equal or greater attention. Single people often focus on the social, financial, and career areas to the detriment of the others, and married individuals likewise are prone to focus on the family, financial, and career areas while giving the others short shrift. When they learn about all seven areas and how they interrelate to form a complete life, a light goes on.

Kelly, about whom we learned previously, had a job to support her financial life but not a real career. Once she understood the difference between the two, she was able to orient her career to support her finances while attaining much higher pleasure and satisfaction. The story of Terri is another example of how understanding the Seven Areas of Life can create a major breakthrough.

The story of Terri (understanding the Seven Areas of Life).

Terri was originally from San Antonio, but when I met her she was living in Minneapolis, Minnesota, and working for a Fortune 50 corporation. She received a very good salary and had a great apartment, a new car, and no debt. Her life, however, was not in the **Happy** quadrant.

When I introduced to her the concept of the Seven Areas of Life, she said, "I guess I haven't spent as much time on my education plan or as much time with family as I would like. That might be part of the problem."

"I see," I said. "If you could spend more time at work or more time with your family, which would you do?"

"Family, definitely," said Terri.

"What would that do for you?" I asked, beginning to guide her up the Ladder of Fulfillment, which we will discuss in a later chapter.

"They are really important to me, so I would be spending more time with the people I love," she said.

"If you could spend more time with your family or spend more time with the people you love, which would you choose?" I asked.

Terri had a great apartment, a new car,
and no debt–but not happiness. GETTING TO WHY

"I see what you're getting at," she said. "I would spend more time with the people I love. All of them."

"And what would that do for you?" I asked, smiling now that Terri's face had lit up with excitement at her discovery.

"That would get me where I need to be in my family and social areas," she said.

"So, that's what's missing?" I asked.

"I think so. I always just assumed that I had to put career first to make money."

"The trick is to get all seven areas in balance," I said. "That's not always easy, but it's certainly worth doing. This is your *life*, after all."

"Right," said Terri. "The big picture is what matters."

Terri and I spent about 30 minutes creating goals in all seven areas, and within one year she had finished an educational program, moved back to San Antonio, Texas, and started her own business. She's now close to her family and friends and has achieved an excellent balance in all the areas of her life. About once a year, she calls me for a tune-up consultation.

You too can achieve this level of pleasure and satisfaction and place yourself firmly in the **Happy** quadrant. The self-assessment on the next page will help you get started in balancing your Seven Areas of Life and managing your life as a whole.

Please perform the exercise for this chapter in the workbook at the back of this book. The entire workbook may also be downloaded in PDF format for free at www.gettingtowhy.com.

Chapter Five

Avoiding the Role Trap

Several years ago I put together a one-act, one-person play in which I depicted the disciple Matthew (the tax collector) and his response to the events of Good Friday and the death of his best friend, Jesus.

An amazing thing happened every time I presented this production: I could not comfortably get out of the character and greet people after the play. I became so involved in the role that I *became* Matthew, and after the lights dimmed at the end of the performance, I would slip out a rear door and go home.

I have seen this phenomenon happen hundreds of times with different "characters": athletes, senior managers, pastors, doctors, attorneys, moms and dads, and so on. All of them playing their roles, all of them on the wrong stage.

When I explain the Seven Areas of Life to my clients, I ask them to rate how they are doing in each area and consider potential improvements. I emphasize that, no matter how poorly they think they are doing in a particular area and no matter how low they score themselves, the Self always deserves a 10 out of 10. Don't define yourself by any of the roles you're playing. Doing so can make you sick. Emotionally, physically, spiritually ill.

Instead, always define yourself as your core person—your potential, which is a 10. The Self is *always* a 10.

I could not comfortably get out of the character and greet people after the play.

The story of Joan.

I once talked with a mother, Joan, who was distraught over the terrible grades her son was getting in seventh grade: mostly D's and F's but with one A in physical education. She believed she was failing her son and was a terrible mother and wife. How embarrassed she would be if friends and neighbors found out how awful she was! Regardless of whether or not she was correct in her assessment of herself as a mother, she was allowing her perceived score in this area—a zero—to be her score for her entire life. She was defining herself completely in her family role.

This story is made even sadder by the fact that Joan had four other children who were all successful in school and in their careers. She was completely defining herself as a bad mother and parent in the Family and Home area and taking all the other areas of life down with it.

I looked at the son's report card and asked, "Are you taking credit for the A in physical education?"

"What are you talking about?" asked Joan. "Of course I can't take credit for that—he did that all by himself."

"If you're taking credit for the F's and D's, then *Why* not the A as well?" I asked.

"I don't know," she said.

"Also, are you taking credit for the successes of your other children?"

"No," she said.

"*Why* not?" I asked.

"They just did well—I've never had to push them," she said.

"But you push your one son, whom you perceive as a failure?"

"No, I don't really push him either," she said.

"Is it fair to say that you're allowing him to make his own choices and live his own life, just as you have with your other children?" I asked.

"I suppose so," she said.

"Then what are you beating yourself up about?" I asked.

"I don't know," she said.

"Maybe you should wait until you understand the reason *Why* you do so before you do it again."

"Maybe you're right," she said.

I would bet that nearly every day or so, most of us define and redefine ourselves in a role, either large or small. Many of us get trapped in this role without a rear door through which to exit. Make sure that you are on the right stage while playing your roles, and remember that the goal is to be a whole person.

Please perform the exercise for this chapter in the workbook at the back of this book. The entire workbook may also be downloaded in PDF format for free at www.gettingtowhy.com.

Chapter Six

Change

Until now, we have dealt with some fairly challenging topics, but now we come to perhaps the most challenging of all: change. There's a reason *Why* this is the longest chapter in the book: its message is the most important and quite possibly the most controversial.

The "CW" on change is dead wrong.

These days, the conventional wisdom is that people don't want change. They are uncomfortable with it. They would rather stay in the present state of affairs forever. But nothing could be further from the truth! Any time people express dissatisfaction about anything—hardly a rare occurrence—they are saying they want change. People want to get better jobs, fix the potholes in the streets, win the lottery, eliminate political corruption, lose weight, go back to school, find a significant other, and so on. People want big changes, small changes, superficial changes, and fundamental changes.

The catch is this: We want change on our own terms—anything and everything that matches our own wants, needs, and ideals and nothing else. The following are what I perceive to be four important facts about change:

1. We all want change—on our own terms.
2. All change causes some degree of grief.
3. Changing the world begins with changing ourselves.
4. We only change ourselves when the benefits of change outweigh the benefits of maintaining old behaviors.

Let's take a look at these points individually.

We all want change—on our own terms.

Any desire of any type is a desire for change. If I'm hungry, then I want to get up and get something to eat—a change—but I want to pick the restaurant. I want my house to be cleaner, but often I don't want to clean it myself.

I want more money, and I'd even like to go out and earn it in a way that challenges me and gives me personal satisfaction—but I don't want this new job to be too challenging, or boring, or distracting from the other things I find enjoyable or meaningful. In fact, I'd like to wake up in the morning for my job only when I'm well-rested and perfectly in the mood for the tasks that lie ahead of me.

All change causes grief.

Buddhism has recognized this fact for millennia in the concept of *viparinama-dukkha*, or the "pain of change." *Why* does all change cause pain, suffering, or grief of some kind? Simply because no change occurs *completely* on our own terms.

For example, I may be looking forward to moving into a new house: it will have more space, a pool out back, a twelve-car garage, and many other amenities that will decrease my pain and dissatisfaction while increasing my pleasure and satisfaction. On the other hand, as we all know, nothing is perfect: the new house may also mean a longer commute to my workplace, a bigger mortgage payment, bigger grounds to maintain, and so on. And, even though I haven't moved yet, I'm already missing my comfortable den with its comfortable furniture and all my favorite books and mementos arranged just so.

If I could accomplish the change of moving *completely* on my own terms, I'd take the new house, keep the old, and have an infinite amount of money to pay for it all. That, of course, is not likely.

We can't lose sight of the fact that, even when we get what we desire most, there will still be moments of grief. Needless to say, a lot of change in life happens in complete contradiction of what we want. A lot of change causes us not just bittersweet emotions, not just a little pain, but a lot of grief.

Changing the world begins with changing ourselves.

No one simply gets up one morning, drives to a random office building, stumbles through a door and lands the job of his or dreams. No one ever improves his or her health by accidentally eating the right foods and doing the right exercises. No one ever heals a broken relationship by drawing Scrabble tiles that just happen to spell out an effective request for reconciliation.

Rather, all positive and effective actions begin with the right thoughts and intentions—in other words, with the right interior state. That's *Why*, in order to change the world, we need to change ourselves first. We all would like positive things just to *happen* to us, and sometimes they do, but we are not in control of such change. Doing things as you are doing them today will, at best, produce a tomorrow that looks like today; at worst, it produces a tomorrow that is completely out of your control.

As Joe Jackson sang back in the 1980s, "You can't get what you want till you know what you want." To produce the tomorrow of your dreams, you must first dream the dream and set the goals. The dream must be positive—good for you, good for the ones you love, and good for the world; otherwise, in the long run, it will not bring you the pleasure and satisfaction you desire.

Getting to *Why* is all about creating that positive interior state; it's all about understanding your dream. What then is required to live the dream? The proper actions based on an understanding of *Who, What, Which, Where, When, How, and If.* One final element is the cooperation of the world, or luck (although through proper planning and effort we may try to minimize the importance of luck).

We only change ourselves when the benefits of change outweigh the benefits of maintaining old behaviors.

We have all known an addict—someone who just wouldn't give up alcohol or drugs despite the fact that the addictive substance was clearly ruining his or her life. The reason *Why* the person wouldn't make the necessary decision to quit the substance is that, to him or her, the perceived benefits of using it outweighed the perceived benefits of quitting. Or, put in a negative way, the perceived grief of quitting was greater than the perceived grief of using.

In our Quadrants of Fulfillment Graph, many people who exist in the **Unhappy** quadrant are unable to do anything but run from pain. In other words, their motivation is entirely of the negative variety. They do not go to the dentist until they have a toothache, they do not consider career options until they are fired, they don't pay their bills until the collector is knocking on their door, and so on. This is somewhat of a caricature, but perhaps the idea will be clear. We all know people who lack the essentials of self-empowerment—the Three-Cylinder Engine of Personal Progress that we will discuss in a coming chapter—and only move when something or someone kicks them in a different direction.

If you are reading this book, then congratulations! You are not counted among the self-disempowered. Before you or I get too cocky about our level of empowerment, however, we should keep in mind that each of us has blind spots in which we are less able to envision and pursue our own direction. For example, when it comes to writing, I am a poor self-motivator and thus teamed up with a highly organized and motivated writer to help me put this book together.

One reason *Why* getting to *Why* is so important is that only by doing so can we escape the trap of a life based on negative emotion. In other words, we should not be running helter-skelter *from* pain and dissatisfaction; we should be marching in an orderly fashion *toward* pleasure and satisfaction. We can only do so by first understanding our interior state, observing how this state influences our actions, and then finally recognizing how the results of our actions cycle back into our beliefs. The Cycle of Change graphic helps make this clear.

The Cycle of Change

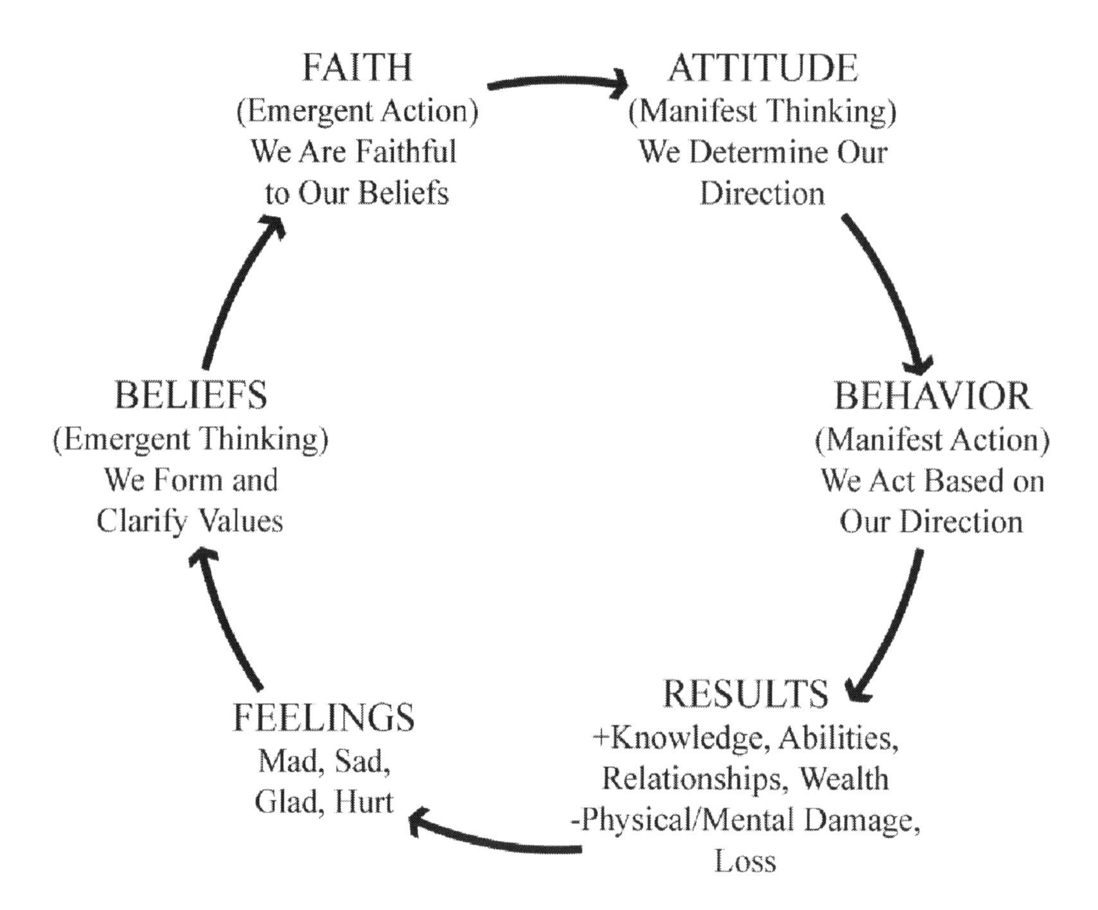

The Cycle of Change.

You can start anywhere on the cycle, but let's start with your feelings about your education. Suppose you are not happy, since a college education is, rightly or wrongly, required for advancement in your industry—and you don't have a college education. You're feeling, in this case, pain and dissatisfaction.

If you go back to school, you believe you'll achieve greater pleasure and achieve a greater sense of satisfaction by being more marketable in your industry. You can see yourself moving toward the upper right quadrant of happiness. You are faithful to your beliefs and enroll in school, buy books, attend class, and so on.

You do well in school, and so your attitude is good. Like the attitude of a ship, it points you in a particular direction, subtly or not so subtly determining your course. In this case, your good attitude spurs you on to beneficial actions. You go through the cycle faster and the results are easy to get. Ultimately, you achieve the degree of your dreams.

What happens, however, if you get a bad grade in your first course? That D or F result could quite likely bring pain and dissatisfaction, altering your belief system. When you are then faithful to your beliefs, your faith and attitude might suffer, resulting in actions that completely eliminate the chance of getting the degree.

There is no place on the cycle where you are necessarily out of control, but at the beliefs and attitude stages, self-awareness is necessary, and, at the faith and behavior stages, self-discipline is necessary to maintain control.

Perhaps the greatest piece of knowledge that human beings have attained in the past 10,000 years is this: we can change. Change for the better, change in a way that can take you to the **Happy** quadrant. At the same time, your ultimate *Why* itself will change. Getting to *Why* is a dynamic, not a static, activity.

The story of Rob and Steven.

I consulted for an insurance company a few years ago. Rob, the sales supervisor was having a problem with one of his salespersons, Steven. He sat down with me and asked for help on the matter.

"Steven's a problem. His numbers have been flat for years. He always makes his quota, but that's it. He just does the bare minimum," said Rob.

"*Why* do you think that is?" I asked.

"It's hard to say, but he's really negative about the company."

"You've heard me talk about change before," I said. "We're faithful to our beliefs, so, unless we know what Steven believes, it will be hard to understand his attitude and his actions."

"Right," said Rob.

"So maybe we should invite him in here and see what he believes," I suggested.

"Good idea," said Rob.

Steven happened to be in the building—not out making sales calls—and we invited him to join the discussion. Reluctantly, he accepted our invitation. Less reluctantly, he began to tell us what he didn't like about the company.

"Yeah, I've been here ten years. In that time, nothing has changed. It's all about the money—more sales, more salespeople. They just come and go. I've stuck it out—sometimes I don't know *Why*. You're not treated like a real person here," said Steven.

"Now, wait a sec," said Rob. "I don't think I'm like that."

"Oh, you're a great guy, to be sure," said Steven, "but the company gets to everyone eventually. I've had five supervisors in ten years. The good guys like you eventually got sick of things and left."

"I see," said Rob.

"What's worse, said Steven, continuing, "is that there's no upward mobility here—no recognition for hard work. Some years I did better than others, but it never made a difference."

We thanked Steven, and I continued my conversation with Rob.

"We already know what Steven's actions are: stagnant effort to sell with stagnant results. But what did you learn about his beliefs, faith, and attitude from the conversation?" I asked.

"He believes that nothing he can do will bring him greater success in the company," said Rob.

"Right. But is he correct?" I asked.

"He is partially correct," said Rob. "The management of the sales department in the past seems to have been pretty impersonal. But, of course, now the company is trying to make all kinds of changes. That's *Why* they're using you as a consultant, right?"

"Sure," I said, "but who's going to prove to Steven that the company is changing?"

"Me?" said Rob.

It's not just Steven who believes this company is cold, calculating, and impersonal; it's a lot of people. GETTING TO WHY

"That's right," I said. "Just like a person, a company has a belief system that it acts on. It's not just Steven who believes this company is cold, calculating, and impersonal; it's a lot of people. The only way to change the company's beliefs is to change each individual's beliefs. To do that, better company behavior is required."

"I see," said Rob.

Rob truly did see, and he immediately began to engage with each of the people he supervised, taking an interest in them as individuals. He spent extra time getting to know Steven, spending about an hour a day exploring his career and personal history. Slowly but surely, Steven began to trust that Rob was sincerely interested in him as a person and not just a rainmaker.

The results were dramatic. Steven's sales numbers showed an immediate improvement, and his new and retained business tripled within in the year. Ultimately, Rob selected Steven as his successor. At the same time, I was working with other departments, guiding newly engaged managers toward a people-oriented corporate environment. Today, the company is extremely successful and is renowned as a wonderful place to work. Both on an individual and organizational level, change is possible. Rarely easy, but always possible.

Please perform the exercise for this chapter in the workbook at the back of this book. The entire workbook may also be downloaded in PDF format for free at www.gettingtowhy.com.

Chapter Seven

Wellness

In our hearts, we know what wellness is. We know that, barring some medical condition or injury over which we truly have no control, we have the power to be well over the long term. To thrive. To feel the glow of physical, mental, and spiritual health. To love and be loved.

Wellness is about a lot more than not being sick. Simply avoiding pain and dissatisfaction is not enough. Rather, we are not well unless we are experiencing pleasure and satisfaction and finding meaning and fulfillment in our lives. To do so, we need to get to *Why*.

When we are not well, it may be that we are choosing to be less than we can be. Let's explore the ways in which unwellness strikes and how we can either avoid it or recover from it.

Avoid the Phoenix Syndrome.

Think about the last time you had the flu or a bad cold. Think about how good it felt to get better after the illness. Of course, we know on a rational level that it's better always to be healthy and never to be sick if we can help it, but, paradoxically, the feeling of getting better can be so good that we seek it out, setting our wellness afire so that we can rise like a phoenix from the ashes. I call this the "Phoenix Syndrome," and I've seen its perverse and tragic effects many times over the years.

Looking at our Four Quadrants of Fulfillment gives us a clue as to *Why* people succumb to this malady. In the Phoenix Syndrome, a person toggles between pain and the center point, mistaking this movement for pleasure or even satisfaction. Eventually, however, the person begins to feel dissatisfaction at that center point—precisely because he or she hasn't gotten to *Why*—and looks for a way out, any way out, and ends up repeating the cycle.

In the previous chapter I mentioned the addict who won't give up alcohol or drugs because the perceived benefits of using a substance outweigh the perceived benefits of doing without it. The "Phoenix Addict" is constantly getting on and falling off the wagon. He gets a DUI, seems to have hit "rock bottom," and then goes to meetings, does everything right, and stays sober for months, maybe even for years. But then he starts drinking again, seems to hit rock bottom again, and the cycle starts over.

The "Phoenix Spouse" crashes and burns in marriages—then rises again (this time it's "true love"!). The "Phoenix Boss" has always just found the *perfect* employee, the one who won't disappoint, the one who won't have to be fired (eventually, of course, the employee gets the axe after "disappointing" or "betraying" the boss). The "Phoenix Entrepreneur" is constantly starting a new scheme, which goes well for a while, then plummets to earth, usually with several investors on board.

Just because someone fails multiple times does not mean he or she is suffering from the Phoenix Syndrome. What sufferers have in common is their fundamental lack of wellness. For example, the Phoenix Boss doesn't just happen to goof up in selecting employees again and again; he or she *desires* the stress of a dysfunctional superior-subordinate relationship and the pseudo-catharsis that arises in the hiring and firing process. He or she has not yet gotten to *Why* and taken the steps needed to avoid the cycle altogether.

Avoid the Phoenix Syndrome. Get to *Why* and embrace your own personal vision of wellness and happiness.

The Cycle of Wellness.

Even if we avoid the Phoenix Syndrome, we are bound to experience periods of unwellness in our lives. The Cycle of Wellness graph helps explain how unwellness strikes and how we can return to health and happiness.

In the center is the constantly flowing River of Change. We desire change on our own terms, and sometime we get our way, but most change does not perfectly match our needs. Thus, we are constantly receiving stimuli that make us feel insecure, putting us on the Bank of Unwellness.

For example, imagine driving on the expressway; here we can literally see and feel the flow of change all around us. As we move along, we experience little moments of insecurity: "Where is my exit? Where am I going to eat lunch?" Nothing is prompting us to act other than our own needs, and we are usually capable of taking care of them without any sort of problem. The bridge back to wellness here is short and sturdy. We cope at this level many times a day.

Suppose we continue driving, and suddenly someone cuts in front of us. It's a dangerous situation, so we experience fear. Now we are prompted to act. The bridge back to wellness here is slightly longer and more tenuous, since our success will depend on our driving skill and strength of nerve, but here again we usually make our way back to the Bank of Wellness.

We can choose to take it to the next stage, however, and get angry at the driver who cut us off. It is normal to experience anger in such a situation, but doing so doesn't help us. The bridge back to wellness becomes longer and thinner still: some people can get over anger fairly quickly, but others fume for hours or even days over small incidents.

The Cycle of Wellness

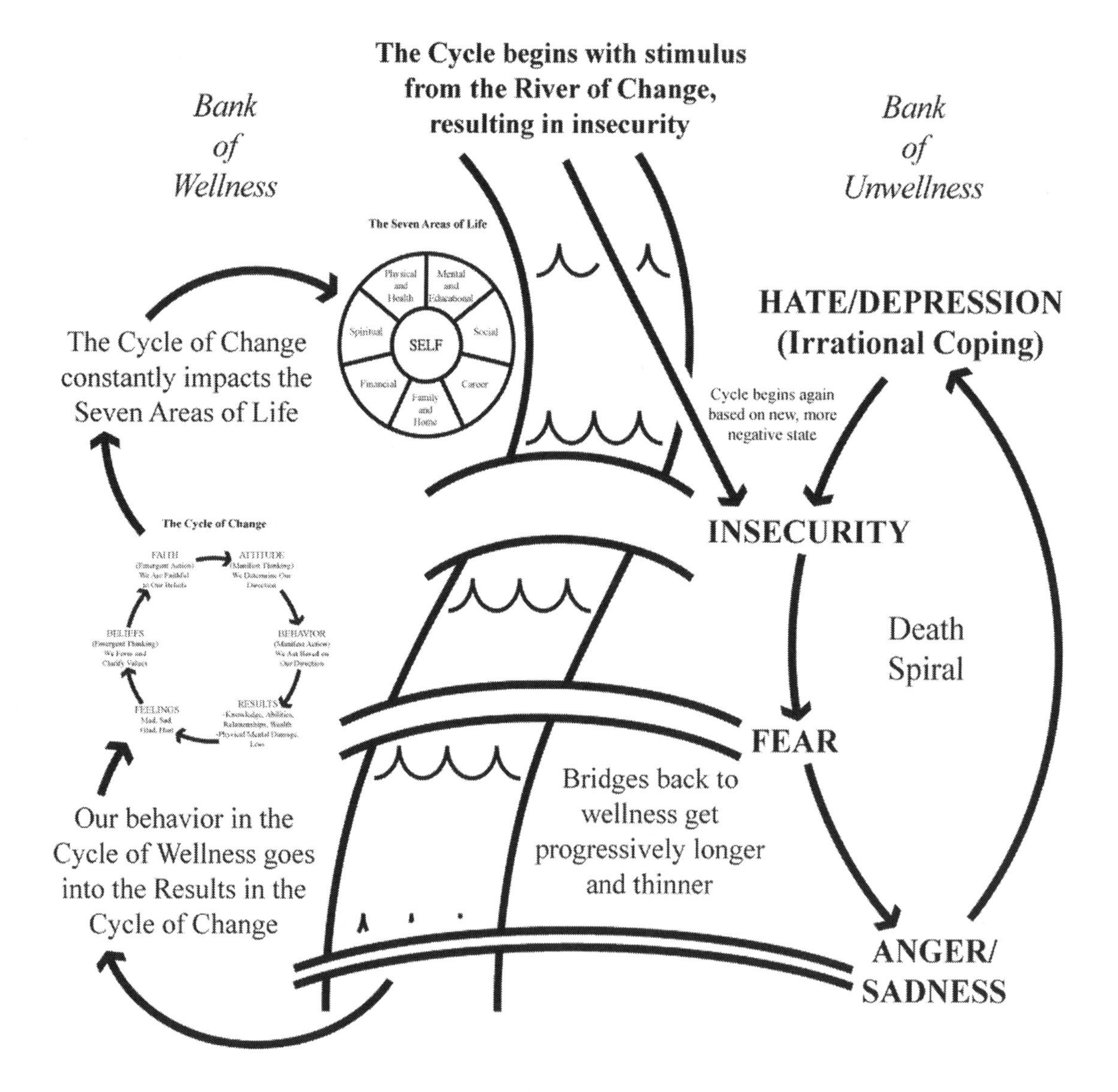

Beyond the Anger/Sadness stage lies Hate/Depression, where we are no longer acting rationally or in our own best interest. For example, we could follow the person who cut us off and, in a fit of road rage, vandalize their car or worse. The bridge back to the other side is now quite rickety indeed, since, at this point, we tend to enter an entirely new reality based on our own highly negative emotions and actions. If, for example, we see a police car pull up after we do something illegal in a fit of rage, we will have a whole new Cycle of Wellness to deal with in which we are not nearly in such good shape as we were just a few moments before.

Moreover, people who have gone all the way to Hate/Depression almost always enter an entirely new social reality. The people who tried to help us during the Fear and Anger/Sadness stages may give up on us. Haters begin to associate with other haters (sometimes literally joining hate groups), and depressed people tend to cut themselves off from others. It is in this new social reality that the next Cycle of Wellness takes place.

Because we are at a disadvantage in the new cycle, we often quickly progress right to Hate/Depression again. Now we are in the Death Spiral, from which it becomes very difficult to extricate ourselves. People in the Death Spiral often end up hospitalized, incarcerated, or dead unless someone intervenes beforehand.

Looking back at our graphic, we [illegible] the left of the River of Change is the Bank of Wellness, which is where we want to be [illegible] even Areas of Life are in pretty good shape. The results from the Cycle of Wellness [illegible] in the Cycle of Change, which constantly impacts our Seven Areas of Life.

Let's consider another q [illegible] le of Wellness. The boss calls us into his office and tells us we're fired. We go [illegible] ur livelihood is at stake. Quite likely we go to Anger/Sadness, too, since we p [illegible] serve to get fired and we're genuinely sad about our failure, even if we didn't des [illegible] ase we go on to experience Depression, finding ourselves unable to get back on th [illegible] nother job. Not working or even looking for work puts us in a worse position bot [illegible] d self-esteem, and a new cycle begins based on the new reality we have created fo [illegible]

On the other hand, maybe at the [illegible] ad it coming. My performance has been poor. Let's take it like an adult and de [illegible] eling angry or sad, negotiate a decent severance package, assess the causes of ou [illegible] cessary steps to succeed in the future.

It's a mistake to think that only negativ [illegible] Cycle of Wellness, since *all* change causes at least some degree of insecurity. [illegible] ting married: the butterflies in the stomach or outright fear that people experienc [illegible] e more than a cliché; as someone who has married hundreds of couples, I can at [illegible] real phenomenon. Further, for some people the joy of marriage is no joy at all, a [illegible] adjust to their new life despite its many positive aspects and fall into depression. A [illegible] job is another ostensibly positive change that can have its pitfalls, too, as when a pe [illegible] he or she will not be able to perform or actually fails in the position.

The Cycle of Wellness does not apply only to individuals. It also applies to couples, families, businesses, and even entire countries. Many times I have begun an intervention at a business only to find one group or more of employees completely consumed by hate for another group or for the company as a whole.

The story of Bob (performing poorly in the Cycle of Wellness).

The following is a story from my life of someone faring poorly in the Cycle of Wellness.

Bob was a pastor whose church I was attending. When I announced I was leaving the pastorate, he encouraged me to serve his church as a regular guest speaker and develop a church school program. Despite the fact that we both respected and liked each other, the honeymoon period did not last long at all.

Bob soon felt Insecurity because of my presence and was absolutely certain that I was going to use the church as a springboard to get back into the pastorate, despite the fact I was busy growing a business. I had conversations with him in which I tried to guide him away from insecurity and back over to the Bank of Wellness. I tried to build trust.

My efforts, however, failed. Seeing that I was popular with the parishioners, Bob became worried about his own position in the church. In the Fear stage, he began to fabricate things about my family and me, telling parishioners and leaders that I had threatened to divorce my wife, who had been diagnosed with cancer, unless she gave up smoking.

Bob proceeded onward to Hate. He sent a nasty letter about me to the superintendent that was full of lies. This move backfired, however, since the letter was so clearly irrational and hate-based that the superintendent ended up moving Bob to a different church entirely. Within two years, Bob was divorced, separated from the church, and living in a distant state. His conflict with me was just part of a larger series of problems that culminated in drastic and negative changes in his life. He was simply unable to extricate himself from the Death Spiral. He could not get well.

The story of Selene (performing well in the Cycle of Wellness).

In her early forties and a very successful salesperson, Selene had attended one of my workshops on communication and wellness and was having a great deal of trouble coping in her current marriage. In fact, her family life was in a shambles.

She was on her third marriage and, even though it was deteriorating into emotional and physical abuse, she still did not want to be known as a three-time loser. Her current husband was handsome but mean, and her previous two selections seemed also to have been based on GQ, not IQ or EQ.

Selene seemed to be going from Insecurity about having three strikes to outright Fear that the people in her life would see her as a loser. I reminded her that in the early stages of the Cycle of Wellness there are a lot of people available to help one, but as one moves from Insecurity to Fear to Anger/Sadness to Hate/Depression, those friends and helpers will start to drop away.

Selene discovered that everyone in her life celebrated the fact that she was exiting a bad relationship.

GETTING TO WHY

It was just a small observation on my part, but for Selene the light went on. She discovered that every single friend and associate in her life celebrated the fact that she was exiting this bad relationship, and they were ready to help her make that change. She abandoned her fears and moved back across the River of Change to great wellness. In particular, her children were elated that their mom was safer, happier, and healthier.

Seek and accept help early in the Cycle of Wellness.

I believe we always have people available to us that will hold our hands and kick our butts at the appropriate time. We just need to let them do it. Asking for help is not a sign of weakness; it's a sign of interdependency, which is actually a sign of maturity. As Thomas More asks in his brilliant book, *Care of the Soul,* "Don't you want to be attached to people, learn from them, get close, rely on friendship, get advice from someone you respect, be part of a community where people need each other, find intimacy with someone that is so delicious you can't live without it?"

We are social animals and will always need help from others in order to create and maintain wellness. Recognizing this aspect of our nature is just another part of getting to *Why*.

Please perform the exercise for this chapter in the workbook at the back of this book. The entire workbook may also be downloaded in PDF format for free at www.gettingtowhy.com.

PART TWO

ACHIEVING WHY

CHAPTER EIGHT

THE LADDER OF FULFILLMENT

In most of the chapters of this book, I'm providing the theory first and then a story to illustrate the theory. In this chapter, I'm reversing that order, and you'll understand *Why* in a moment. Then, in the following chapter, I'll be presenting one of the most powerful tools in this book.

The Story of Jamie.

Jamie was a salesperson for a large manufacturing company. He was very outgoing, charismatic, and interested in life. He was successful to a degree, keeping himself and his family comfortable, but he would only sell to a certain level of client and would rarely go after the big dog. I was asked to take a look at situation, since it was believed that Jamie was capable of performing at a much higher level.

One day I was listening to Jamie and his sales manager have a conversation about his performance: how many cold calls he made, how many clients he visited, how many prospects he closed—all the classic sales stuff. I observed that Jamie had no quarrel whatsoever with what the manger was telling him; rather, he nodded his head in agreement, answered the manager's questions, and provided no original input as to what might be going wrong in his career.

Later, I asked Jamie how he felt about the conversation.

"It's nothing new—we go through this every month or two," said Jamie.

"You seem to be agreeing with your manager's assessment of your performance," I said.

"Well, results don't lie. I'm above average but not great," said Jamie.

"You seem to be enthusiastic about most things in life," I said. "Enthusiasm is a great selling tool. Do you have that high level of enthusiasm when you sell this company's products?"

"I think I do," said Jamie. "I just seem to be talking to the wrong people a lot—the non-decision-makers."

"*Why* does that happen?" I asked.

"Because I make it happen," said Jamie.

"*Why*?" I asked.

"I guess I feel I'm not in the same class as the C-level execs," said Jamie.

"What you're saying is that you don't mind rejection so long as it doesn't come from the top decision-maker?" I said.

"Wow, I've never thought of it like that," said Jamie.

"As I said, you're so enthusiastic, communicative—you like to talk to people. What would you really like to do?" I asked.

Jamie pondered for a moment before answering. "I guess I'd really like to own my own business."

"What would that do for you?" I asked.

At each race Jamie encountered something he had never really thought about: portable toilets.

GETTING TO WHY

"It would give me more freedom," said Jamie.

"Which would you rather have: your own business or more freedom?" I asked.

"I would rather have more freedom," said Jamie.

"What would that do for you?" I asked.

"I wouldn't have to defend my behavior and performance to others," said Jamie.

"Which would you rather have: more freedom, or not needing to defend your behavior and performance?" I asked.

"More freedom, I think," said Jamie.

"What would that do for you?" I asked.

"I could choose my own products, prices, and customers," said Jamie.

"Which would you rather have: more freedom or the ability to choose your own products, prices, and customers?" I asked.

"I'd rather choose my own products, prices, and customers," said Jamie.

"What would that do for you?" I asked.

"It would give me more flexibility and more opportunities," said Jamie. "Right now I'm selling hammers, so to speak, and everything needs to look like a nail."

"I see," I said. "Not to be repetitive, but which would you rather have: more flexibility and opportunities or the ability to choose your own products, prices, and customers?"

"The ability to choose my own products, prices, and customers," said Jamie.

"What would that do for you?" I asked.

"It would give me variety in my life," said Jamie.

"Which would you rather have: the ability to choose your own products, prices, and customers, or more variety in your life?" I asked.

"Variety," said Jamie, this time with greater confidence.

"What would that do for you?" I asked.

"That's just what I want," said Jamie. "Flexibility. Variety. Doing things my way. That's what I really want." Jamie's eyes had a new fire in them.

"What could be your first step in achieving that?" I asked.

"I could run a marathon," said Jamie. "I've thought about that before."

"How would that help you in achieving your goal of flexibility, variety, and autonomy?" I asked.

"It would demonstrate my discipline, endurance, and perseverance—the things I would need to succeed if I had my own company. I could prove I have what it takes," said Jamie.

"Fantastic!" I said. "When would you like to run your first marathon?"

"Within six months," said Jamie.

"Better get started then!" I said.

What happened next was truly amazing. Jamie bought a great pair of running shoes, found a track he loved to run on, and started keeping a log of his performance. He did run his first marathon within six months, and soon he was doing marathons on a regular basis.

At each race he encountered something he had seen before but had never really thought about: portable toilets. He hadn't known there were portable toilets with changing stations and portable toilets for handicapped people.

Jamie had found a product that inspired him! The fact that most people aren't inspired by portable toilets and don't give them much thought gave him the opportunity to create a niche for himself. Within a year of deciding to run his first marathon, he had quit his job and started his own portable toilet business, which before long he grew to number two in the state (no pun intended). He is now happy. He's gotten to *Why*.

How the Ladder of Fulfillment works.

I call the method of questioning and answering illustrated in the story of Jamie the "Ladder of Fulfillment." In the next chapter, you'll answer the questions for yourself. You can do the exercise with a friend or simply ponder the answers yourself and write them down.

At each step of the ladder, you make a choice between something of importance to you and what that important thing can do for you. These choices form a chain that inevitably leads you to what is *most* important to you.

Further, the chain always leads to a final answer that is abstract in nature. For example, Jamie wanted flexibility, versatility, and autonomy. Other people might want to help others, become famous, find love, and so on. The chain, however, does not give you *only* an abstraction: along the way, you'll also familiarize yourself with the specific methods that are right for you in finding fulfillment.

Understanding your highest level of fulfillment is important, since there are many ways to fulfill an abstract goal. For example, suppose your highest level of fulfillment in life is helping others and nursing is your preferred method of fulfilling that goal. Even if you cannot become a nurse right away, you can still fulfill your purpose through a variety of means. In Jamie's case, he could not achieve full autonomy immediately, but training for a marathon was a step that he could take then and there.

Avoid the "Please No More Pain Pitfall."

When I go through the Ladder of Fulfillment with my clients, I often encounter a certain type of response.

"What is a goal that is important to you?" I ask.

"Financial freedom," says my client.

"What would that do for you?" I ask.

"I wouldn't have to worry about money," says my client.

"Which would you rather have: financial freedom or no worries about money?" I ask.

"Not having to worry about money," says my client.

"What would that do for you?" I ask.

"I could then just relax and really live my life," says my client.

What the client is saying in this case is that he or she would like to get at least to zero on the Pain-Pleasure axis and is not even thinking about achieving higher satisfaction. I call this the "Please No More Pain Pitfall." We hurt so bad in one or more of the Seven Areas of Life that we can barely imagine what it would be like to be fulfilled.

To avoid this pitfall when you go through the Ladder of Fulfillment, it can be helpful to rephrase the first question in this way: "What is an important goal for me, assuming that I have eliminated the major sources of pain in my life?"

Begin finding fulfillment today.

As we saw in the story of Jamie, going through the Ladder of Fulfillment exercise doesn't just lead us to a clear vision of fulfillment; it also gives a clue as to what we can do immediately to achieve it.

Too often in life we become fixated on a goal that is neither our highest purpose nor something that leads directly to it. Take again the example of desiring "financial freedom." Of course, having a lot of money usually helps us in achieving our goals, but fixating on making money can be a hindrance if our true highest purpose is actually helping others. It may be possible to enhance your Career Area of Life to make ends meet while simultaneously starting volunteer activities that genuinely fulfill you. To give another example, if starting your own business is your chosen method to achieve autonomy, then you could perhaps stay in a job that is not your ideal while starting a business on the side that provides true satisfaction and fulfillment.

Finding happiness and fulfillment isn't something you do after you have a million dollars in the bank and all of the mundane problems of your life are solved. Rather, the process starts with understanding your highest purpose and acting upon that understanding in the here and now. The simple fact is that we almost always have to get on the Ladder of Fulfillment somewhere in the middle instead of jumping right to the top. The important thing is not getting stuck in the middle of the ladder.

Please perform the exercise for this chapter in the workbook at the back of this book. The entire workbook may also be downloaded in PDF format for free at www.gettingtowhy.com.

Chapter Nine

The Three-Cylinder Engine of Personal Progress

Life slants downhill, so unless you're putting effort into moving uphill, you're sliding. The proof of life is death. Death only comes to things that are alive.

That's a negative metaphor, so let me offer a positive one. The only time a pilot has to apply the full power of the aircraft is on takeoff. The rest of the time, less power is required. Once you get to *Why* and attain cruising altitude, you're in good shape. You can pull back on the throttle a little bit.

Break the momentum of doing nothing.

We have to break the momentum of doing nothing. We have to challenge the status quo that we create for ourselves and take action.

Metaphors aside, we all know that, if we lie in bed all day, the world will still change without us. We need to get up, take a shower, make some coffee, go to work and take care of business, come back home and take care of our families, clean house, arrange our finances, and do a myriad of other things or life will fall into disorder. That's what I mean by "life slants downhill." On the other hand, we can establish systems for ourselves through which we take care of business and find fulfillment in the process. That's what I mean by "cruising altitude." Life can be tough, but life can definitely be all we want it to be if we approach it in the right way.

I said all metaphors aside, but here is another, and I promise it will be the last one I introduce in this chapter. In order to make personal progress you need an engine—an internal combustion engine with three cylinders:

Self-Motivation

Goal Direction

Positive Attitude

Unless all three cylinders are functioning, you will not get where you want to go. Consider the cases in which one of the cylinders is missing or not functioning well:

Goal direction is missing. You are a wanderer with good attitude and lots of motivation. You take shots with no aim, since your target is missing, and you keep starting over every few days, weeks, months, or years.

Positive attitude is missing. You have a goal clearly in mind and you are actually taking steps toward the goal, but your self-doubt and negative attitude are clouding the process. You're going in the right direction with bad fuel in the system.

Self-motivation is missing. You're leaning in the right direction with a great attitude but no action. You are positive and happy about the possibilities–you just won't take steps to begin the process.

We've all known people who fall into one or more of the above conditions. We've all probably spent time in each of them ourselves. Can you imagine what life is like when *all three* of the cylinders are missing or not functioning? One ends up floating face down in the ocean of hopes and wishes (yes, that's another metaphor, but let it pass).

When all three cylinders are firing, however, we are almost unstoppable. The following three stories illustrate how we can repair a broken cylinder and get back on the road to success.

The story of Steve (overcoming a lack of self-motivation).

My good friend Steve is brilliant and holds a master degree in economics. He had his own real estate appraisal business, but there were so many unethical people in the field that he walked away from a very successful enterprise. He held himself to a higher standard than his competitors and found it difficult to compete when others were fudging their numbers to please people in need of higher valuations.

Steve pondered how he could best use his strongest skills: analysis and evaluation. For years he had been receiving a newsletter about commercial real estate. The company that produced the newsletter was making millions of dollars, yet Steve believed with good reason that their product offered only one tenth of the value that he was ready to provide. Despite this belief, Steve never could work up the combination of self-motivation and self-confidence—or "mojo," as he called it—to create his own newsletter. Newsletters were something the big boys did, not a "little guy" like him.

One day Steve shared with me his dream of creating a newsletter, and the self-motivation cylinder began to fire. Now that he had gotten to *Why*, we immediately began working on *What* and *How*. Within 30 days, we developed his business plan. Within a few more months, his newsletter was up and running. Within a year, Steve was operating the successful business of his dreams.

The story of my dad (overcoming a lack of positive attitude).

My dad was notorious for seeing the glass as half empty. Sometimes he'd put forth a special effort and make the glass completely empty, even when it was not. For example, we'd go together to my high school basketball games, and he'd proclaim with great sadness and certainty that our team was going to lose. "They're done! Game's over," he'd say—even in the first ten minutes of the game!

My dad had great goal direction and superior self-motivation, yet, owing to his rotten attitude, he would constantly criticize processes that he or others successfully employed in any project. Moreover, the gloom and doom he generated blinded him to the successes that he and others achieved.

My dad was successful in spite of his poor attitude because he was so determined and focused. He used to make beautiful pieces of cherry furniture that were just spectacular. But he criticized the shape of the wood and the pieces he made—nothing was ever A-OK. For a local church he once built a beautiful 5'6"-tall solid cherry cross with perfect bevels and all. The first thing he pointed out to me about this masterpiece was the imperfection on the back that would be impossible to see once the cross was installed in the church.

Dad seemed to be coachable at times. The first time I ever swore in front of my dad I was 16 years old. I had come home from my basketball game, and I was feeling pretty pleased with my play that evening. As soon as I walked in the door, however, my dad, who had gone to the game and gotten back before me, said, "You passed off too much, you didn't shoot enough, and you missed some rebounds."

"Darnit!" I said, although that was not the actual word I used. "Can't you ever tell me I did something right?"

Interestingly enough, my mother said, "Don't swear at your father." She didn't disagree with the comment itself, just the particular word.

This happened to be a weekend in which there were games on both Friday and Saturday night. After I got home from the next night's game, in which I felt I had not played very well at all, my dad said, "I thought you played a pretty good game. But you passed off too much, you didn't shoot enough, you missed some rebounds, and I don't think the coach played you enough."

It was the same list but with a positive beginning and an extra complaint! I walked up to him and said with a hug, "Nice try, dad!"

My father's greatest gift to me was my appreciation for life-long learning. In the late 1950s, he became interested in radio and TV repair and took several home correspondence courses in this area. He began working with a local television and repair group, and the owner of the local radio and TV store offered to make him partner. At the same time, his company offered him a position as a supervisor in their heat treating department, which was the world's largest. He couldn't do both, so he chose the security of his current company. Over the next decade, he immersed himself in classes and earned a degree in metallurgical engineering. He eventually became department superintendent, attaining a level of success that even he could not dismiss or downplay.

By seeing my father study and take tests day after day and night after night, I learned that lifelong learning is both possible and effective. My mother's contribution to my growth in this area was her frequently and confidently saying, "You can be anything you want to be and do anything you want to do if you want it bad enough." I didn't doubt it then, and I don't doubt it today (the only caveat is that goals must be attainable, as we shall see in a later chapter).

The story of JB (overcoming a lack of goal direction).

Some people are always bouncing around like a frog in a hailstorm. They have a positive attitude. They have the self-motivation that leads to action—a lot of action. Yet, lacking goal direction, they're running in several different directions at the same time.

Sometimes the problem is that they have too much talent and get distracted by all of the things of which they are capable. Sometimes they are afraid of digging too deeply into any of the possibilities that are open to them: after all, trying too hard to make it in any one area could lead to failure. And smart, capable people never fail, right?

Until my coauthor Matt came along and virtually forced me to get started on and keep working on this book, I had dreamed of writing it but simply wouldn't sit down and do so. I had written and published numerous articles. I had created many successful workshops. Yet I had found it impossible to act on my dream of helping people through a book like this one.

I incorrectly saw writers as sedentary people—not men of action like Byron or Hemingway. Perhaps I was afraid that the book would not be as compelling as the lectures and workshops that I had been offering and succeeding with for years.

Some people are always bouncing around
like frogs in a hailstorm. GETTING TO WHY

Matt's enthusiasm and abilities were the catalyst that allowed me to write the book you are reading right now. Which just goes to show that even people who help others self-actualize sometimes need help themselves, and we should never be too proud to accept the help we need!

Please perform the exercise for this chapter in the workbook at the back of this book. The entire workbook may also be downloaded in PDF format for free at www.gettingtowhy.com.

Chapter Ten

Self-Esteem

Self-esteem can be one of the most positive personality characteristics—and one of the most destructive. Healthy self-esteem and self-worth are crucial to one's success in life. The trick is to avoid the extremes of self-worship and self-depreciation and find the happy medium: a realistic appreciation of one's own talent and potential.

Proper self-esteem is essential to getting to *Why*. How can our destination be worth reaching if we don't believe we deserve to reach it? On the other hand, if we esteem ourselves unrealistically or too highly, then we may find that our achievements are a figment of our imagination or have required too great a cost.

Extreme No. 1: The Self-Worshipper.

At one end of the spectrum, we have those persons who esteem themselves higher than God: they are arrogant, self-indulgent, self-righteous, self-important, and just plain rude.

Already a few faces have probably come to your mind. Self-Worshippers often get farther than they should in life because their dominance allows them to fulfill the qualifications of manager—on a superficial level.

Once Self-Worshippers have found positions in an organization, they will do whatever it takes to achieve success on their terms, leaving dead and dying relationships along the way and destroying others' self-worth and success. Such destructive managers can be very difficult to get rid of, owing to their hiring practices. They usually hire one of two types of subordinates: fellow Self-Worshippers or Milquetoasts.

Self-Worshippers that only hire other Self-Worshippers do so because they believe that self-worship is a sign of strength, and they wish to reward the strong. In such a case, the scorched earth syndrome will be even worse. The organization descends into chaos as the arrogant battle for supremacy, and there is constantly a game in progress of "Who's In, Who's Out?" Eventually, the leader and his favorites run out of people to use and abuse, and the death spiral of the company continues.

More common are Self-Worshippers who only hire Milquetoasts, doing so because they want to be in complete control of everyone who works for them. Such bosses eventually push everyone out of the organization who will not pledge absolute obedience. Although Milquetoasts can be competent workers, eventually the lack of anyone to stand up to the boss catches up with the organization. Another bad side effect of a Self-Worshipper hiring Milquetoasts is that, when the boss goes on vacation or even simply leaves for a short period of time, the Milquetoasts will fail to make decisions, since they've not been empowered to do so.

There is little good news to offer when it comes to Self-Worshippers: they are quite common in the world of business, and their influence is large and negative.

Extreme No. 2: The Milquetoast.

At the other end of the self-esteem spectrum we have the Milquetoasts: self-effacing, self-limiting, and almost completely powerless in their own minds.

Initially, Milquetoasts evoke compassion in the people they work with, but eventually their colleagues and subordinates get tired of always having to build them up and serve as their therapist. In general, Milquetoasts make awful managers, since standing up for their own ideas is extremely difficult for them. In many cases, they "earn" their position as manager by working at a firm for a long time or by inheriting it in a family business.

In customer service, Milquetoasts can sometimes succeed, since they will do whatever it takes to satisfy the customer. Even here, however, one must be careful, as they will give away the company by over-satisfying customer needs and responding to customers who are in fact not sincere.

The good thing about Milquetoasts is that they are relatively scarce as bosses. The bad thing about them is that they are quite commonly encountered as the annoying toadies of Self-Worshippers.

The worst of both extremes: The Gutter Ball Champion.

One piece of good news to offer about Gutter Ball Champions, or GBCs, is that they are rare compared to Self-Worshippers and Milquetoasts. The second piece of good news is that their nature is to retreat when they fail, so they eventually go away (only to pop up elsewhere!).

People of this unpleasant type have all the pride of a champion bowler, yet, when they throw a gutter ball in life's lane, they simply discount the event by saying, "Whoops! I'm no darn good," without making any commitment to improve their game. Lacking true accountability, they often say, "It wasn't my fault. The conditions were not right. You expected too much." Yet they will repeat their poor performance again and again with the same exaggerated self-worth and lack of consideration for the consequences of their actions.

GBCs typically gain their sense of entitlement early in life: they are born with high intelligence or great talent in music, sports, or any area that allows young people to outdo their peers. Adults heap praise on them; peers look on in admiration. The feeling that they are *just better* sinks into the psyche, never to be eliminated.

When things are going well for GBCs, they look down upon the Earth as if they own it. When things are not going well, they crawl into a hole, doing their best to escape the repercussions of their actions. Admitting failure is enough, they think.

The behavior of Gutter Ball Champions can be quite maddening to the people around them. When the moment comes to say, "Ah hah! You're not quite what you thought you were, are you?" there is no payoff to enjoy as there is when true Self-Worshippers fall from their perch. There is no soul-searching to observe, nor much in the way of an apology to receive.

The story of Roger (overcoming self-worship).

Roger was 30 and wanted to go into the pastorate. He felt called by God to preach and lead others to God. His feeling of having been called, however, had not led him to humility and compassion but instead to obliviousness of other people's ideas, attitudes, and feelings.

Indeed, since God had called him, he didn't need any other advice. He was smart enough, bright enough, wise enough, and ordained enough to be a successful pastor. Teaching, coaching, and mentoring were tasks beneath his stature. He felt, rather, he should be preaching to thousands and saving sinners en masse. He even mentioned that world salvation was probably nigh due to his ministry.

Roger had always been a winner in the things he had done in the past. Thus, he had been chosen to be a winner for God, and, with the Supreme Deity on his side, he was certain to succeed.

Our denomination asked me to be Roger's teaching elder. I finally was able to help him dial down his arrogance, narcissism, and huge ego by recording our conversations. I also recorded his sermons, which were good in many ways but also contained large doses of fire, brimstone, and other accusatory messages designed to frighten listeners into following his theological path.

Listening to his own sermons was eye-opening to Roger. I asked him to imagine himself in the pew, unable to respond. Roger was able to hear the arrogance, the aloofness, the condescension, and the accusatory and judgmental comments that his sermons contained. In short, he was appalled.

Eventually Roger asked me, "How do I change?"

"You've just started," I said. "Anyone willing to ask that question is already on the road to change. I would first recommend that you learn how to listen. I've got some exercises that I believe can help you."

"I'm willing to do that," said Roger.

The transformation took about a year with a significant shift occurring in the first few weeks. In order to hone his listening ability, Roger instituted a feedback session after the church service. During this time, he would listen to members' comments and refrain from talking himself until asked a specific question.

With the Supreme Deity on his side, Roger was certain to succeed.

GETTING TO WHY

This initiative was a big success, and soon 100 people or more remained after services to ask questions and dialog with each other about the message. Over time, Roger became an expert listener. Today, he is an extremely successful preacher in Florida with a congregation of more than 1,000 members.

Self-assess—and, if needed, get therapy—to achieve proper self-esteem.

Self-Worshippers are notorious for their inability to see that they self-worship, but Roger serves as an example that it is indeed possible for some. Although the exaggerated confidence of Self-

Worshippers sometimes helps them get ahead, most would be even more successful if they could find a middle ground, since their arrogance and narcissism turn people off on a consistent basis.

Escaping the Milquetoast mindset is also difficult. It's a well-known fact that bad experiences in childhood can have a large, long-lasting, and negative effect on self-esteem. Sometimes therapy is necessary to transcend one's past and get a fresh start.

Diagnosing personality disorders and treating psychological problems is beyond the scope of this book, but if one of the profiles strikes a chord in you, make a personal commitment to change and get help if you feel you need it.

If, like the vast majority of people, you have normal to slightly low self-esteem, understanding the Areas of Life and going through the exercises in this book will help put your life in perspective and give you a helpful boost of self-understanding, self-awareness, and self-esteem.

Please perform the exercise for this chapter in the workbook at the back of this book. The entire workbook may also be downloaded in PDF format for free at www.gettingtowhy.com.

CHAPTER ELEVEN

SAYING "NO"

Getting to *Why* means not only finding your highest purpose but also discovering what *isn't* your highest purpose. It's a fact of life that you cannot do everything you'd like to do, much less everything that everyone else would like you to do. One convenient tool in eliminating the paths you choose not to pursue is the word "no."

I tell people that "no" is a complete sentence. "No" may be augmented, however, by other phrases that comfort the requesting or demanding party:

"No for now—ask me later."

"No, thank you."

"No, but that's interesting."

"No, but good luck!"

"No, but I'll pray for you."

Too often we use the phrase, "No, I can't." Please don't say this. You've just sold the rights to your decision to someone else. When a "good salesperson" hears you say can't, he or she will immediately employ tactics to help you say, "I can." For example, a car salesperson has nine different ways to convince you that you can afford a particular vehicle. Most people don't know what their total debt is; they only know their monthly payments. Not saying "no" will put you deeper in debt—in multiple ways.

Just say "no"—no arguing, no convincing necessary.

This one little word can be very hard to say; most of us have experienced such an inability. At the same time, however, we tend to admire those people who can say no in such a way that we respect them. Do you know such a person? Do you value your own opinion? Then become that kind of person. Nothing is stopping you!

The story of Betty (learning to say no).

Betty was a mother who came to me for counseling about her two daughters. They were not doing as well in school as they were able, they were ignoring curfews, they were talking back to their parents, and they were dressing inappropriately in school and in public. This may sound like typical teen rebellion, and to a certain extent it was, but there were also signs that the girls might get into more serious trouble if their parents could not regain some degree of control over them.

One day Betty and I discussed strategies to take back the reins.

"People learn what you teach them," I said.

"Are you telling me I've taught them to behave this way?" said Betty.

"A parent is a big source of this type of behavior. When is the last time you said no to your girls and really meant it?" I asked.

Betty thought for a moment but couldn't come up with a recent time she had said no.

Berry's two teenage daughters were getting out of control.

GETTING TO WHY

"*Why* are you afraid of telling your girls no and meaning it?" I asked. "Backing up the 'no' and following through on what you say."

"I'm afraid they will hate me," said Betty.

"What your daughters hate is authority and accountability. They're learning from you that they can challenge authority and win," I said.

"I suppose you're right," said Betty.

"The first step is to go into their rooms and take all of the clothing you deem inappropriate, box it up, and hide it. Two, as soon as they get home in their car, you take the keys. Take their transportation and unique look away for immediate effect. For them to reacquire these things, they'll have to demonstrate respect for authority and accountability," I said.

"Okay, I'm with you," said Betty.

"Now let's talk curfews," I said. "Based on what you've said, their curfew will be 10:00 on weekdays and 12:00 on weekends. If they are late a minute, they'll have to give back ten minutes the next night. If they're late the next night, then it's 20 minutes for every minute. If they're late the third night, then it's 30 minutes. And so on."

"Oh dear, that won't be easy," said Betty.

"I doubt it will," I said. "Now, when you say no, look them in the eye and don't say anything else. If they start to talk back or complain, just walk away, smiling as you do. You're not playing this game on their terms any more."

Betty implemented all these measure, and at first she had a real battle on her hands. The girls screamed bloody murder when their beloved "outfits" were taken from them, and enforcing the curfew was a nightly ordeal. In the first two weeks, one of the girls was late so often that her curfew one night was 6:15 pm.

It took about a month for the girls to realize that they had a new mom. During this time, they learned how to communicate with their parents, respond to their expectations, and negotiate when they truly wanted something.

These girls are now in their thirties with girls of their own, and it's amazing the number of times they have thanked their mother for teaching them how to say no and hold their ground. Mom earned the respect and love she wanted by saying no and having firm rules, and her daughters have carried on this tradition.

Please perform the exercise for this chapter in the workbook at the back of this book. The entire workbook may also be downloaded in PDF format for free at www.gettingtowhy.com.

Chapter Twelve

Fear and Doubt

My goal in this chapter is to provide a few key concepts that can help you put your fears and doubts in perspective so that they can't prevent you from getting to *Why*.

The world's biggest killers.

My years of serving in Vietnam and working as a counselor and consultant have taught me that fear and doubt have killed more people than war or disease and destroyed more businesses than financial crises or managerial incompetence. Fear and doubt are also your greatest enemies when you are trying to get to *Why*.

As Frank Herbert said in his *Dune* series, "Fear is the mind killer." It also does a job on the body. I have seen dozens and dozens of people go into hospitals, be diagnosed with life-threatening illnesses, and nevertheless walk out healed and healthy. I have also seen people receive not-so-threatening diagnoses and fade away in months, weeks, and sometimes days. You can guess which were the fear and doubt victims and which were not.

Fear and doubt are your greatest enemies when you are trying to get to *Why*. GETTING TO WHY

Doubt is the uncomfortable place between certainty that something is so and certainty that it isn't. We doubt the truthfulness of our friends and colleagues and the loyalty of our spouses—with or without cause. Worst of all, we doubt our own worth and abilities. We doubt our power to overcome the travails of life, including illness.

A 54-year-old husband and father of four I knew was diagnosed with testicular cancer in July at a world-famous clinic. He came home, went to the attic, and pulled out the daybed on which his father had himself died of cancer. Putting the daybed in the corner of the family room where his father had put it, he lay down and died in November of that same year. He actually had died on that fearful and doubtful July day; it had simply taken a few months for his body to catch up.

We human beings are very good at fearing and doubting in irrational ways. The single most dangerous activity in which we engage on a regular basis—driving a car—does not cause us any fear at all, yet the thought of speaking in public paralyzes us, even though doing so poses virtually no risk. As we shall see in an upcoming chapter, fear is the number one reason that people do not set goals.

Most children are free from fear and doubt—at first. In time, fear and doubt come from parents, teachers, and other well-intentioned adults who impose filters, or ways of seeing the world, on children. Instead of exhibiting fear and doubt only in specific circumstances, children end up feeling these negative emotions all the time. Then they pass on their irrational modes of fearing and doubting to their own children, perpetuating the problem.

The first step in overcoming fears and doubts: write them down and talk about them.

Fear and doubt are at their most powerful when they are locked away in our minds. They feed on our silence and on our shame of revealing them to others. Even though we know we'll feel better once we talk to someone about our fears and doubts, often we hesitate to do so. The philosopher Nietzsche said that the most intimate things are the most common. In other words, we discover that those thoughts and feelings we assume are only ours, reside only within us, are actually feelings and thoughts common to many other people.

Let's take the first step. Right after you finish this chapter, get a notebook and write down every fear and doubt that you have. If you fill one notebook, then start on another. Once you have written down all your fears, you'll have gained a new power in life: the power to say with confidence, "This is what I fear, nothing more."

Next, find someone who will listen skillfully and compassionately to the fears and doubts that you have written down. This person may be a friend, a relative, a spiritual counselor, a life coach, or a therapist. It's up to you, but it's crucial to find a true listener.

Once you have written down and told someone about all your fears, inevitably they will have less power over you. For some people the reduction will be small, for some it will be great, but there *will* be a reduction, and taking these steps *will* make a difference that you can feel.

After taking these initial steps, you can evaluate what fears and doubts are still remaining. Perhaps nothing more will be needed. If you still suffer from extreme fear and doubt, make sure you get the help you need. For those with chronic, uncontrollable anxiety, medication may be necessary.

We can't eliminate all risk; we can only do our reasonable best.

I often feel that there is a hidden, pervasive, and incorrect assumption in our culture these days: namely, that if we eat the perfect diet, exercise the perfect amount, and otherwise maintain the perfect lifestyle, then we won't get sick and die. Or, at the very least, we will at least live to be 115 or more.

We see this assumption revealed in the media's reporting on medical studies, in which suddenly the talking heads are frowning upon saccharin or trans fat or the latest verboten substance, as if we could eliminate every single risk factor from our lives and achieve perfect health and immortality.

Needless to say, immortality also requires perfectly safe automobiles and homes, the elimination of all pollutants, and so on. Plus, bicycle helmets. We can't forget those.

My over 50 years of solid research (your results may be different), indicate that we do not get out of this life alive. Despite our best efforts, we're all going to die, and many of us are going to be done in by genetically caused diseases that medical science is powerless to do anything about.

I'm all for eliminating the big risks to healthy lives and pursuing wellness. Nevertheless, I believe that focusing too much on small risks, as the media are prone to do, has the perverse effect of making us more fearful, not simply because we end up with more things to be afraid of but also because we end up believing that protecting ourselves with such precision is something we can and ought to be doing—all of the time.

We should all have a good, realistic plan for our Health and Physical Area of Life. We should implement it and not be afraid. When we get sick, as we inevitably will, we should go to the doctor and get treatment.

And so it is in each of the Seven Areas of Life: when we have a plan, are implementing the plan, and are regularly revisiting the plan, then we are doing our reasonable best, and we should work on overcoming and controlling our fears.

The story of Vicki (overcoming fear and doubt).

One of the most powerful examples I have ever witnessed of overcoming fear and doubt was my wife Vicki. In March 1986, she was diagnosed after two and half days of a bad headache with glioma multiforma: a malignant, inoperable, and 100% fatal tumor—a spider of cancer in the brain. At age 34, she was facing death. We had been married twelve years, and our children were eight and ten years old.

During the first few days that Vic stayed in the hospital—the first of many times—we talked about the kinds of things that were important for us to experience before the end. Amazingly, her only concern was that I would remarry after she was gone.

I knew the origin of this concern. In our second year of marriage, she had asked me the Year Two of Marriage Question: "If you had to do this all over again, would you get married?"

"Heck no!" I had responded. "This marriage thing is hard work. If I'd known how tough it was to do this while going to school and starting a career and raising a family, I would have put it off for sure." (This was one of the stupidest things I have ever said in my life.)

"*Why* is it important for me to remarry?" I asked Vic, sitting next to her bed in the hospital.

"The kids need a mom," she said.

"Whoa, I said. Not a good idea. After the kids are grown, I'll be stuck with the kids' mom. We didn't get married to have children. We got married to have a life together for 40, 50, or 60 years." But then I said, "I will remarry," I said. "Not for the kids, and not for you. I'll remarry *because* of you. You've made being married absolutely wonderful, and I want more of it. I know where that question came from. I regret what I said in our second year of marriage. You have changed my mind and my beliefs."

Vic smiled and was absolutely content. Her fears and doubts were gone. That's all she had wanted, since, to her, getting to *Why* meant giving pure, unconditional love that I could never earn but only receive.

Over the next two and half years, she was constantly active, immersing herself in exercise, reading, meditation, and doing all the things she could to keep herself as healthy as possible.

One day we were having a conversation about our philosophies of life, and the topic of winning and losing came up. I stated the truism that we choose to win or lose in life.

"No," Vic said, looking at me with an expression I'll never forget: completely resolved. "Some winners don't have choices. If I don't win, I die."

Some winners don't have choices. I have taken great inspiration from these words ever since, using them in my life as a mantra against fear and doubt.

Although Vic went through many examinations and many treatments in those two and a half years, when the end came, it came suddenly. On July 22, 1988, she had her first seizure. Over the next ten days, she would have 6,000 more.

The end came on August 1. Vic had had a flat EEG for about seven hours, and I said to the doctor, "Things aren't going to get better, are they?"

The doctor said, "No, this is it."

I then told the doctor, "I know how this equipment works, and I will do what you cannot." It was just the two of us, alone. Holding her hand, I felt her last breath, and her last pulse came at 1:30 pm.

Please perform the exercise for this chapter in the workbook at the back of this book. The entire workbook may also be downloaded in PDF format for free at www.gettingtowhy.com.

CHAPTER THIRTEEN

GOALS

Napoleon Hill famously said, "A goal is a dream with a deadline." After you have climbed the ladder of fulfillment and identified your highest purpose, floating up near the top rung will be several dreams. These are your goals.

For example, you may have identified "helping people" as your highest purpose, and "becoming a heart surgeon" as your long-term goal, which entails "getting into medical school" as your near-term goal.

If we don't put deadlines on our goals (and the objectives that we need to reach to attain our goals), then we won't make a sufficient effort to attain them. Worse, we may completely use up the time in which we *can* achieve them.

Goals are all about the big picture. Objectives are smaller-picture and more precise. For example, in order to get into medical school, you will have to pass the MCAT; in order to pass the MCAT, you will have to study; in order to study for the MCAT, you will have to buy study materials, and so on. You will also have to do well in high school and college and achieve high GPAs.

It's possible to split hairs as to where goals end and objectives begin, but the important thing is the process:

1. Identify your highest purpose through the Ladder of Fulfillment.
2. Identify the dreams/goals that support your highest purpose.
3. Set objectives to attain your goals.

Another way of looking at goals is as paths to wellness in the Areas of Life. For example, the goals of losing a specific amount of weight and becoming able to run a specific distance in a specific amount of time could increase your wellness in the "Physical and Health" Area of Life, while the goal of reducing your credit card debt to zero could increase your wellness in the "Financial" Area of Life.

Here again we must keep in mind that we don't achieve true wellness merely by avoiding pain and dissatisfaction but by achieving pleasure and satisfaction and true meaning and fulfillment. That's why I said in our chapter on "The Ladder of Fulfillment" that it's important to avoid the "Please No More Pain Pitfall." Ultimately, one's goals should all support achieving one's highest purpose in life.

How many goals should one have?

My rule of thumb is that one should always have at least one goal in each Area of Life and no more than three. I have found that, in almost every case, if one has more than three true goals (i.e., fairly big dreams) in an Area of Life, then there simply is not enough time to complete them all.

The exception to this rule is a true linear progression involving several large steps over a long period of time. For example, one may plan to run for a local office, then run for congressperson, then run for senator, then run for governor, then run for president. It would be unwise, however, to attempt concurrently to become a world-renowned heart surgeon and president of the United States.

Fear and doubt are *Why* most people don't set goals.

For a long time, management experts have recognized that there are three types of fear that prevent people from setting goals: fear of failure, fear of ridicule, and fear of success—in that order. Recall in the last chapter when I said that fear and doubt are the biggest killers of businesses? They're also the biggest killers of goals.

No one likes to fail, so the easiest way to avoid failure is simply not to try in the first place, right? I once held a goal-setting meeting in which a man literally ran out of the room, screaming, "You're not going to make *me* fail!" In a way, that kind of reaction is understandable. Accepting the status quo of our lives entails the least risk. Yet we cannot get to *Why* if we do not embrace the fact that not everything in life will turn out as we desire.

The fear of ridicule is easily understood. When you proclaim that you are going to do something great or make a big change, there will always be people walking around with a pin to puncture your balloon. They can only be big by making you feel small, since they are afraid of your potential success. *Why?* There are many possible reasons, but one common fear is that success will take you away from them.

An additional comment I make concerning the fear of ridicule is this: Never share your goals—I repeat, *never*—never share your goals with someone unless you are *certain* that they will support you. Did I say *never?* Never do so!

It may sound absurd, but people can also fear success. They may not desire the extra responsibility or pressure that success entails. For example, if they succeed, then they fear that the internal or external expectation will be simply to do more, immediately. Both companies and parents are notorious for failing to celebrate a success before raising the bar yet again. "Good job—now go do better," is their ineffectual method of motivation.

Other people may not believe they deserve success. This self-destructive philosophy will not allow a person even to set a goal, let alone fail at a goal.

If your goal is moral and ethical, and if you've put the kind of thought behind it that I've recommended, then it's better to try and risk failure than never to try in the first place.

The story of Bill (setting goals).

Bill, a representative of a major life insurance company, knocked on my office door one day and said, "You're that goal-setting guy, aren't you?"

"Sometimes," I said. "What can I do for you?"

"I need to work on my goals," said Bill. "I have a feeling they're inadequate."

"I see," I said. I asked Bill how he had heard of me, and it turned out that one of his friends had attended a seminar of mine. Bill had decided to drop in without an appointment since he'd found himself with some extra time on his hands that day. Lots of extra time, since he'd scheduled no appointments at all. We were off to an interesting start.

"So, in what area do you need to improve your goals?" I asked.

"My monthly sales are not what they should be," said Bill, "so let's start there."

"Okay," I said. "What's your sales goal for this month?"

"To make more than I did last month," said Bill.

"What did you make last month?" I asked.

"Nothing," said Bill.

I offered to shake his hand, and I held on very tight while I said, "Congratulations—you're meeting your goal. Your goal was zero, and you have and are achieving it."

Bill was about 40 years old. In the past, he had worked for an office supply company doing in-house sales. There are two kinds of salespeople: eagles and vultures. The eagle goes out and kills something. The vulture waits for something to drop dead in front of it. It is sometimes difficult to turn a vulture into an eagle, and, in the first phase of his career, Bill had been a vulture for 15 years. Nevertheless, I was willing to help Bill give his eagle wings a workout and begin the second phase of his career. I continued with my questions.

"So, Bill," I said, "how long have you been selling life insurance?"

"Five years," he said.

"How is it going for you, moneywise?" I said.

"Well," he said, "I'm about $20,000 behind on my draw. My manager is starting to get on my case pretty bad."

"Do you mean to say you're about to be fired?" I said.

"Yeah, and about to be broke, too," said Bill.

"That's an emergency situation," I said, "so let's get down to business. First, I need to know how much you need to make every month in order to live. I need to know every bill, how many times you eat out—everything. Also, there are two things you need to avoid doing here: going broke and getting fired. In order to prevent both of these, we'll need to set a firm deadline for achieving your goal."

It is sometimes difficult to turn a vulture into an eagle.

GETTING TO WHY

Bill answered my questions, making his goal *specific*. He now had an exact dollar figure in his mind. And he had his deadline.

"What is the average dollar amount of insurance you sell? How much commission do you earn?" I asked.

Bill provided these details, confirming that his goal was *measurable*. Not only was the figure he required each month measurable in dollars and cents, but the number of signed contracts he needed to obtain each month was also clear.

"Bill, what system are you going to use to keep track of how many cold calls you're making, how many referrals you're getting, and so on?"

Bill and I talked about the system he would need to keep his goal *trackable.*

"Bill, do you have the training, certifications, and knowledge required to sell?" I asked.

Bill said yes, indicating that his goal was *attainable*, meaning that his goal was in concord with his personal reality (physical state, mental state, abilities, skills, etc.).

"Bill, how many hours a day are you available to sell insurance? Is there anything holding you back right now?" I asked.

Bill indicated that he had plenty of time to sell. Nothing impeded him. His goal was *realistic*, meaning that his goal was in concord with his external reality.

I then said, "Bill, I'm going to meet with you twice a day for five days: 7:30 to 8:00, then 5:00 to 5:30. During those 30-minute sessions, you're going to make phone calls to make appointments. I'll coach you on your delivery as you go, if needed."

It turned out that Bill didn't need much assistance. His inside sales experience had helped him develop an appealing and effective phone manner. By simply sitting with him and holding him accountable, I was able to help him get started. He got over 100 appointments in the next two months. I helped him with his sales presentation a bit, and he became an extremely effective closer. Within 90 days, Bill became the top salesperson in his organization. Within a year, Bill became area manager and had three people working for him.

It's amazing what a new perspective can do sometimes. Bill had possessed the talent to be great at his job all along. The concepts I provided to him were simple but had a tremendous effect on his life.

SMART.

SMART is an acronym for Specific, Measurable, Attainable, Realistic, and Trackable. These are the elements that all goals should have to help ensure that they can be realized. By the way, they are also in the order of their likelihood to become stumbling blocks. For example, a lack of specificity is the No. 1 cause of goal failure, a lack of measurability is No. 2, and so on.

Business consultants have been using this acronym for decades with the letters standing for various things, but the above is my version of it, based on helping literally thousands of individuals set and realize their goals.

Let's take a look at each of the elements in turn.

Specific. "To have a good life" is an unspecific goal. So what would make you feel your life is good? "Become rich"? This is also unspecific. How much money would you need to feel rich? When our goals are not specific, then we have no way of knowing whether we have accomplished them, and we have no way of knowing how to accomplish them. In contrast, a specific goal inspires specific actions to accomplish it. The success is in the details.

Measurable. "To have a body that looks like that of a professional body builder" is a goal that can be quite specific as a picture in your mind, but it needs to be backed up by measurable qualities and quantities. You can start working out and looking in the mirror to see the effect, but it will be very difficult to know what kinds of exercise and diet will help you achieve that look. On the other hand, if you know what weight, body fat percentage, and muscular dimensions you wish to achieve, then you have a much better chance of achieving the look. You are developing the measurable components of your goal.

Attainable. Attainability is about whether we have what it takes, mentally and physically, to achieve a goal. I am all for positive thinking, but when we lack—completely and undeniably—the abilities, skills, or qualifications needed to attain a goal, we need to face that fact. For example, at my age and with my level of talent, there is no way that I can become a professional basketball player. It simply isn't going to happen. If we embrace a goal that is not attainable, then we set ourselves up for failure.

Realistic. Realism is about whether external circumstances permit you to attain the goal, the most important of which is time. For example, if your goal, as measured, requires more time, money, or resources than you possess, then it is not realistic.

Trackable. This element is about keeping score. If you are playing a game of basketball and you agree on the measurable components—one-, two-, and three-point baskets—you now have the increments necessary to keep score. A basketball player may score 20 points, yet his team may have lost the game. The score helps us know whether we are winning or losing.

Thinking in terms of SMART is the first part of my system of setting and achieving goals. The second part is using the Getting to *Why* Goal Planning Worksheet.

Guide to the Getting to *Why* Goal Planning Planning Worksheet.

(The worksheet is located in the workbook at the back of this book.)

The Getting to Why Goal Planning Worksheet puts everything you need to plan a goal in one place. Feel free to get messy with the sheet, writing in the margins and using extra sheets of paper as needed. This is a worksheet to get your neurons firing and your hand scribbling—*not* a formality to be neatly filled out, filed away, and forgotten!

Let's go through the sections one by one:

Area of Life. Fill in the Area of Life that this goal will affect the most. At any given time, we should have at least one and usually no more than three goals in each of our Areas.

Today's Date. The date that you start to fill out the sheet.

Target Date. The date by which you wish to achieve the goal.

Achievement Date. The date on which you actually achieve the goal.

SMART. The next five areas give you the opportunity to confirm that your goal is specific, measurable, achievable, realistic, and trackable. The first section is the one in which you write out the goal in the most specific, clear, and concrete way you are able.

Reality Check. In the SMART section, you've identified and described your goal in fairly rich detail. Now you're ready to take a step back and ask yourself these three key questions to confirm whether the goal is really a good one for you at this time.

Fears. As we learned in an earlier chapter, fear is a major reason *Why* people don't set goals and *Why* they fail at goals. Writing down your fears immediately cuts their power in half—give it a try, and you'll be amazed. As you jot down your fears, also write down ways in which you can overcome them.

Benefits. You are going to achieve your goal because it has benefits to you—they are the *Why* of the goal. It is important to write them down, since keeping them in mind will help motivate you and keep you focused.

Affirmations. Here you can write down several affirmations, which are sentences that boost your confidence and help you retain focus. A good way to compose an affirmation is as if the desired goal is already true: "I have achieved my sales quota for the year." "I have $1,000,000 in the bank." "I have found the love of my life." "I am in my dream job and the boss loves me and my work." And so on. They are a great way to summarize your goal and keep your eye on the prize.

Action Steps. These are the actual things you're going to do to achieve your goal. It's good to write them in rough chronological order, with the first step first. You might not use all ten slots; on the other hand, you might fill up several pages with a detailed plan. At this point, feel free to be crude and messy, since getting even just the basics down on paper is immensely empowering. "Target Date" and "Achievement Date" have the same meaning as described above. "Review Date" refers to the date on which you'll assess your progress on this particular step.

Possible Obstacles/Solutions. Here is where you ask yourself to expect the expected and imagine the unexpected. For example, a possible obstacle to your career goal of owning your own business could be the objection of your spouse. A possible solution to this could be creating a presentation for your spouse to show that the business is a viable idea.

I need you to trust me on this: filling out at least one goal worksheet for each of your Seven Areas of Life will empower you as you would not believe. So long as your answers are sincere, even very crudely filled out sheets have enormous value. It really does seem to work like magic: the moment you fill out a sheet, things start to fall in place to make your goal a reality.

Of course, practice makes perfect. The more you work on your goals and your worksheets, the easier it gets and the more detailed your answers become. Your thinking about goals gets sharper, and you get in the habit of doing little things at opportune moments to complete your action steps.

I cordially invite you to fill out your first sheet and see amazing things happen!

Please perform the exercise for this chapter in the workbook at the back of this book. The entire workbook may also be downloaded in PDF format for free at www.gettingtowhy.com.

Chapter Fourteen

Self-Succession Planning

Over the last several years, I've been helping a lot of companies with succession planning, which we'll deal with in detail in the final chapter. Succession is nothing more than delegation taken to its extreme: the delegator delegates completely, leaving the business.

I'd like to advance the concept of *self-succession*, a process in which you succeed to the new you with a new *Why* while orchestrating a smooth departure for the old you.

The first step in the self-succession process is realizing when the new you has arrived—or is trying to arrive. When you pay attention to how you feel about what you do and that feeling isn't comfortable, satisfying, exciting, fulfilling, engaging, or just plan enjoyable, your inner self is trying to tell you something: get back to *Why*. The feeling needn't be negative, however: sometimes you can have a desire or a dream that you just can't shake, that inspires you and enlivens you. A new *Why* is calling.

The following is the story of one the biggest transformations I have undergone in my life. *Why* called and threw me for quite a loop.

The story of JB (realizing when the new you has arrived).

Let me share a prayer with you that I have developed over the past half-century. The earliest version of it came to me when I was twelve: "God help me."

I used this prayer for things like tests in school, Boy Scouts, basketball, track, 4H, and other activities when I felt I needed some extra help or felt a little panicked.

Over the years, the prayer has evolved into its current version, and I do not pray it unless I am absolutely prepared for the answer. It's a form of releasing myself to other options and considerations for my life direction. It goes like this:

Dear God, open the door you want me to go through and forgive my resistance,
and shut the door you don't want me to go through and forgive my insistence. Amen.

After working as a dentist and in other medical capacities in the Navy, I entered college with the goal of earning my DDS. It seemed to be the obvious career choice and I'd been accepted to dental school. Yet, despite the fact that I had worked toward this goal for twelve years, the feeling that something was amiss was gnawing at me. In order to find the right path for myself, I prayed the above-mentioned prayer.

The message that came to me was immediate, simple, and unmistakable: *Become a minister.*

"A minister?" I said back, incredulous. *A minister!*

I rejected the idea, but I had asked for the door to be open, and there it was—open. The instant I shouted, "No way! I've worked for twelve years for this moment!" it felt as though thousands of needles were ripping through my body. I threw every unbreakable thing in my apartment, and sweat poured off me.

I was furious, and I tried to fight back and fight the pain. Of course, resistance was futile. After 20 minutes of this, I threw myself down on the couch and yelled, "Fine! We'll do it *your* way!"

The shower of pain stopped immediately as if I were being told, *You've accepted the door.* An interesting side note: I had run earlier in the evening, and I always weigh myself after showering. I showered and weighed myself again after this painful and sweaty ordeal, and I was amazed to discover that I had lost eight pounds in 20 minutes. Obviously, it had not been a fair fight, but at least my hip wasn't dislocated.

Although I did and still do interpret this experience as a literal calling from the Creator, you are free to interpret it as the manifestation of a new *Why* calling from deep within me. When you feel the call in your own life from whatever source, be prepared to pay attention—and be prepared for some surprises.

The day after my "shower," I went about the task of changing my major from pre-med, pre-dent to pure biology and political science so as to finish school as quickly as possible with a degree that could help me in my new career. When I talked to the guidance counselor about my plan, he jumped up and told me I would make a great pastor. I then talked to old and new friends and told them I was not going to dental school and was going into the pastorate. To my surprise, they supported me fully in my decision and didn't find it odd at all.

It felt as though thousands of needles were ripping through my body.

GETTING TO WHY

I walked home from campus that evening, confident and happy about my decision. Within a week, I met my future wife. Then I held on for dear life.

The harmony of my new Self and my new *Why* stayed with me for 13 years. I could easily fill a book with stories about what I encountered and learned. Leading training, resolving conflicts, helping people deal with death and dying, celebrating births, working with for-profits and not-for-profits, handling legal issues—I covered it all.

I made it through many experiences that tested my strength and understanding of reality. I knocked on the door one evening of a mother who had called, saying she was angry and going to kill her children. When I opened up the door, she had a shotgun aimed at my face. Another time, I was in the delivery room with a 13-year-old. Her parents had thrown her out, and she had no one to be with her, so I held her hand as she gave birth.

In time, however, yet another *Why* called me. When I had my first inkling of it, I said my prayer. This time, however, my marching orders did not come to me instantaneously. Over the course of my final year in the pastorate, I patiently waited for my new Self to take shape.

One day a parishioner came to me and said, "You've really helped me and my family improve communication and resolve conflicts. Now I'm using those same techniques with my executive team. It works just as well there." He owned a large company with 800 employees.

"That's great," I said. "It doesn't surprise me that it works. After all, a company is just like a big family. Or ought to be like one. The same tools apply."

"Well, I could use some more help," he said. "Could we do some team building together?"

In that moment, the image of my new *Why* at last fully coalesced for me. The parishioner and I ended up working together for two years, and I fell in love with being in the trenches with multiple levels of employees, assisting them in their implementation of their company's missions—in other words, helping them align their personal *Whys* with the company's *Why*. Since then, my *Why* has continued to evolve yet remains fundamentally on the same track.

The steps of self-succession.

Here are the steps you'll need to take to bring about your own self-succession:

1. Feel or sense the call of your new Self and *Why*. Are you feeling a major disturbance in your life? Are you dissatisfied even though things are going well on the surface? Does fulfillment elude you for a reason you can't pin down? These things may be signs of the call.
2. Write down your current understanding of your new *Why*, your new mission. Think about it and absorb it. Walk around it.
3. Establish initial goals to fulfill this new mission (see previous two chapters).
4. Begin delegating the functions of the old Self (use the Getting to *Why* Delegation Worksheet we will introduce in an upcoming chapter).
5. ASK—ask yourself whether you have the Abilities/Attitude, Skills, and Knowledge to take on your new *Why*. Start acquiring anything you need to build or modify the vehicle—you—that will contain and transport this new *Why*.
6. Stay focused and review each of these steps frequently.

Once you understand the concepts involved, self-succession is mainly a matter of listening, sensing, and feeling.

Please perform the exercise for this chapter in the workbook at the back of this book. The entire workbook may also be downloaded in PDF format for free at www.gettingtowhy.com.

Chapter Fifteen

Your Personal Legacy

As we discussed in the last chapter, in life we are very likely to pass through several Selves and *Whys*. Each of these Selves will have a legacy that it bequeaths to the future you and the people in your life. Moreover, at the end of your life, you will have a final legacy by which you will be remembered.

The question to ask yourself now is, "What kind of evidence will I leave that I was here, and will that evidence match up with what I wanted to leave?"

This question is not only for people with grand titles: you don't have to be called doctor, lawyer, professor, or president. You can be mom, dad, grandpa, grandma, teacher, school bus driver, or janitor. You can be anything and still leave a valuable, one-of-a-kind legacy.

Giving time helps you leave a powerful legacy.

One of the key ingredients of a legacy is the time you give to people. I have a new doctor in my life named Doug, and one of the first things I noticed about him is that he gave me more time during my appointment than I usually received from physicians.

After my second annual physical with him, I told him that I appreciated the extra time he took with me to talk *with* me and not just at me or about me.

"You probably have fewer patients per hour than the average doctor," I said. I happened to know that the average time a doctor in the US spends with a patient was six minutes. "Since we're talking billable time, how does taking extra time with each patient work out for you?"

"Several years ago I sat down and looked at my entire patient load," said Doug, "and I decided how much time each patient needed or wanted, with a minimum of ten minutes. I have found that this produces the best overall outcome for my patients while keeping the numbers for my practice healthy too."

Doug is in the process of leaving a powerful legacy as a physician. His generosity with time not only improves his odds of understanding his patients' needs; it also sends a message of caring that people are not soon to forget. Similarly, if you truly live and breathe your mission, you will find yourself giving more time to the people with whom you interact. If you give more time to the people with whom you interact, you will find yourself truly living and breathing your mission. Giving time is a major contributor to getting to *Why.*

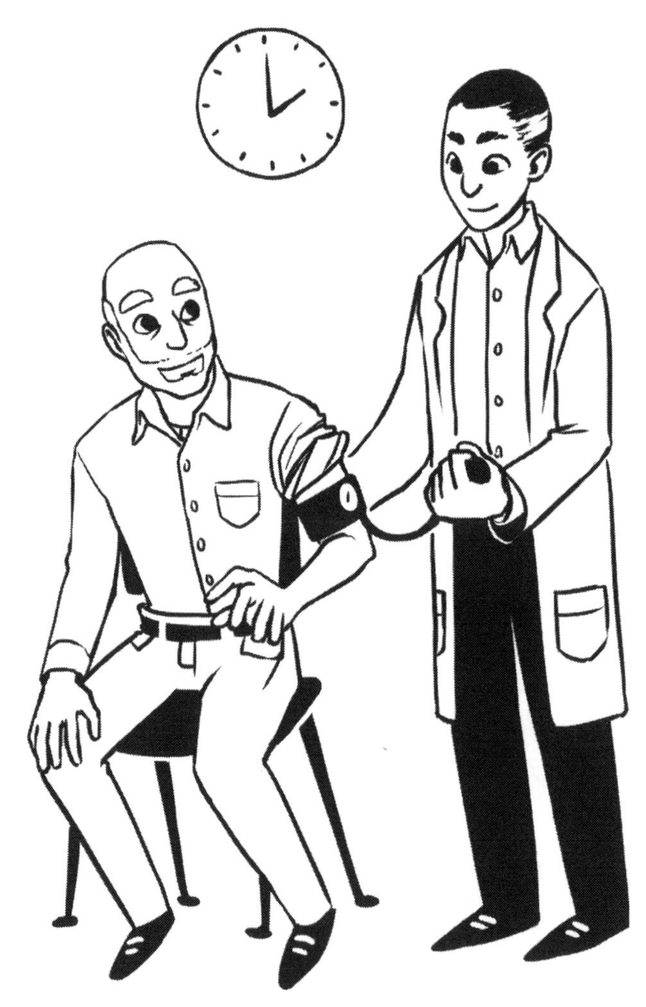

Doug is in the process of leaving a powerful legacy as a physician.

GETTING TO WHY

Selflessness helps you leave a powerful legacy.

The vast majority of powerful and *good* legacies are built on love and selflessness, not pride and ego. Usually, builders of great legacies are surprised when their accomplishments are held up for praise.

A rabbi once told me a wonderful story. God was particularly happy with a man named Josiah, who had continually done kind and helpful things for others all his life. Josiah was getting late in years, and God said to him, "Josiah, I am pleased with you and will grant you your fondest wish. What do you desire?"

Josiah thought for a bit and said, "When I do good for people, I wish never to know that I have done so." God was so pleased with Josiah's request that He granted it to all mankind.

What a wonderful thought Josiah had! Too often in life, however, we're not like Josiah. Not only do we want to know the good we've done right away; we even want to know the payoff we'll receive ever before we've done the good deeds.

Great legacy builders are consistent in their behavior: they care about *all* people, regardless of their state or status. They do the good deeds that they do to benefit others, not themselves.

The legacy of your favorite teacher.

Think of your favorite teacher—he or she will usually spring instantly to mind. What grade or class did he or she teach, and how old were you? I have a tie for first place: Mr. Owen, my high school track coach and psychology teacher, and Mrs. Steepleton, my senior year English teacher.

Here is what they had in common with each other and, I bet, your own favorite teacher: they were tough, firm, fair, and consistent, placing high expectations and demands on every student. At least once a semester, these teachers would give their students, regardless of their current grades, one-on-one motivational pep talks that always conveyed how much the teachers believed in the students and their abilities to do better. In short, they cared.

Now think of your worst teachers. Here's what they all had in common: they were tough, firm, fair, and consistent. This looks like the same list as above—with one huge exception: the worst teachers offered very little to no personal contact. Your favorite teachers *cared.* They cared about you, your work, and your future. Your worst teachers, although they behaved similarly, gave very little evidence that they cared about you or your success.

Here is the lesson to be learned from the legacy of your favorite teacher. I have met a lot of leaders, managers, parents, and government officials who back away from being tough, firm, fair, and consistent because they're worried that doing so will make them less likable. Yet they are wrong. In fact, being weak, lax, unfair, and inconsistent only causes them to be disliked, and their lack of real caring is the final nail in the coffin of their legacy.

Don't be afraid to be tough, firm, fair, consistent, and *caring*. Embodying these qualities gives you the chance to be as admired and respected as your favorite teacher. You could end up someone's favorite manager, parent, friend, pastor, rabbi, or teacher.

Thus, to build a powerful legacy, you need simply do the following:

1. Get to *Why* and begin fulfilling the mission you were meant to fulfill.
2. Give of your time generously.
3. Be selfless.
4. Be tough, firm, fair, and consistent.
5. Care.

Without fail, you will have a substantial and positive impact on others that will be remembered long after you have departed this world.

Please perform the exercise for this chapter in the workbook at the back of this book. The entire workbook may also be downloaded in PDF format for free at www.gettingtowhy.com.

PART THREE

SHARING WHY

CHAPTER SIXTEEN

SYNERGY

"Synergy" comes from the Greek word *synergos*, which means "working together." People and organizations work together effectively when they share the same purpose and goals—in other words, the same *Why*.

Much has been written about this vaunted concept over the years, and often the focus has been on the different *things* that people or organizations can bring to the table. For instance, if you've got a plow and I've got a horse, then we can combine forces to do some farming. If, however, you want to plant corn and I want to plant wheat, then our *Whys* are different, and our synergistic combination of resources is fruitless.

In many a corporate merger, the combination of talents and resources looks good on paper, but the *Whys* fails to coalesce. Indeed, instead of the whole becoming greater than the sum of the parts, it becomes less, and often the new entity sinks with such clattering, groaning, and gurgling as to rival the tragic end of the *Titanic*.

We needn't look to such large-scale disasters to know what happens in an organization when synergy is lacking. Marriages often fail because the *Whys* of the would-be life partners are not in alignment.

When we are able to share *Why* effectively, however, we can accomplish great and powerful things. The following story provides some clues as to *Why* some partnerships and teams work and others don't.

Byron and his Percheron draft horse, Doc (realizing synergy).

One of my father's best friends was Byron, who had very few boundaries in his life and was willing to try just about anything. Some of the stories he and my dad told were amazing and, if true (as I believe most of them were), dealt with things that would get people thrown in jail these days.

One of Byron's passions was raising draft horses: those huge, thundering, big-footed equines that pull wagons and carts and carriages. Today, perhaps the most famous breed of draft horses in the United States is the Clydesdale, known for its relationship with Budweiser, but the Percheron was once the most popular draft horse in the country.

Byron's all-time favorite horse was a giant black Percheron named Doc. Doc was the largest horse I have ever seen in my life. Well over six feet at the withers (i.e., the shoulders), he could easily pull a 7,000-pound sled by himself.

Byron used to enter Doc in horse-pulling contests at county and state fairs. In one type of contest, two horses are yoked together, hitched to a sled weighted with concrete blocks, and challenged to pull it down a 100-foot course. If the horses make the "full pull," more weight is added to the sled, and they go down the course again. The last team to make the "full pull" is the winner.

Watching such contests is a very powerful lesson in synergy. The horses are not whipped down the course or in any way coerced: *they* are competing, and their desire to win can be smelled in the air. Further, one can see in their body language the joy when synergy is at work—and the frustration when it is not.

There is a wonderful story about two massive draft horses in Alaska that were considered the strongest horses in the land. Folks wanted to know which was the strongest, so a contest was set to have a pull-off between the two. The horses pulled and pulled. More and more weight was added until at last one horse was victories. Each had pulled over 9,000 pounds by itself!

But then the folks wanted to know how much weight they could pull together. People bet that, together, they could pull between 18,000 and 25,000 pounds. The actual result was over 40,000 pounds! In this case, the whole was indeed greater than the sum of the parts.

How is it that horses that can pull about 9,000 pounds apiece can pull over 40,000 pounds together? The secret is that they completely mere their power. They breathe and step and pull with such perfect timing that when one horse is exerting its full strength, the other horse is getting a tiny rest. These micro rests let the horses greatly increase their stamina and more than double the amount of weight they can handle as two separate individuals.

Yet here was the problem with Doc. It is critical that horses in a pulling contest be as closely matched in strength as possible or they will not pull evenly and in rhythm. Further, the weaker horse often ends up "pulling in the hole," jumping and lurching and trying to keep up. Byron spent over ten years trying to find a match for Doc. He never did.

Byron spent over ten years trying to find
a match for Doc.

An interesting thing about the weaker horses that Doc pulled with was that at the end of the pulls they were always more frustrated and lathered up than Doc—yet they had done far less work.

Synergy isn't just about piling up strengths.

When dream teams come together, they often leave a lasting imprint on the world. That's *Why* we remember fondly the Boston Celtics of the 1960s and 1970s, the New York Yankees of the 1950s and 1960s, the rock band Cream, the songwriters Rodgers and Hart, and the comedians George Burns and Gracie Allen, just to name a few terrific, synergistic teams.

But synergy can be funny: sometimes teams of less talented people are far more effective than would-be "dream teams," since two or more strong individuals can have ego clashes or simply find themselves unable to make their talents work together. On his own, Doc was the strongest of horses, yet he was not good at partnering with others and fared poorly in pulling contests. Similarly, some people are quite strong on their own yet fail to "play well with others" in some dimensions or perhaps all dimensions of work and life. Such people shouldn't be condemned, however—they just need to find a job and a career in which their individuality is a plus.

When you look to match yourself with others, make certain beforehand that you or one or more of your teammates will not be "pulling in the hole"—or worse. *Why?* More is at stake than mere success. Companies, families, and couples can still be successful even when they are not particularly synergistic, yet the individual team members can find themselves hating their jobs and feeling great frustration because of the lack of synergy. Sometimes they hide behind the outcome of success, using it as a salve to soothe their dissatisfaction. For example, compare the early Beatles to the later Beatles. At first they really enjoyed playing together and created great records. Later they disliked being together so much that they never played live, and they recorded their parts separately in the studio. They were still making great music, but they were miserable. They had synergy at the beginning, but not at the end.

If you find yourself still waiting for the right to come into your life, then it's important not to give up, give in, or settle. It really bothers me to hear people say, "It's not what I wanted, but it's good enough." All too often, when someone accepts second-, third-, or fourth-best, they live with it unhappily—forever. Hold out for synergy.

Please perform the exercise for this chapter in the workbook at the back of this book. The entire workbook may also be downloaded in PDF format for free at www.gettingtowhy.com.

Chapter Seventeen

Trust

Trust is the feeling that people around us have our best interest at heart and are telling us the truth. Trust allows us to relax and just be ourselves: we don't have to waste energy on protecting ourselves because other people have our back.

Can you remember being a child and having an adult swinging you through the air or tossing you up and catching you? You laughed and smiled because you just *knew* that this person you trusted would not let you hit the ground.

Have you ever fallen asleep in a car while your friend drove on through heavy rain? You could relax because you trusted in that person's abilities and wakefulness.

In a marriage, you feel trust when your spouse says he or she is going somewhere and you don't think twice about it. In a company, you feel trust when your supervisor says you'll get a raise if you achieve certain goals and you can count on that statement.

Trust is a complex state of being that is difficult to achieve and easy to destroy. It has both a logical side and an emotional side. We mentally process people's words and actions and decide whether we can trust them or not. Yet, at the same time, we experience trust in a deeply emotional way, as we did when we were children tossed up in the air.

No organization, however large or small, can establish and maintain wellness without trust, since people will neither be able to be at their best nor share a common *Why*.

Trust is a three-legged stool.

It's helpful to think of trust as a stool with three legs: communication, cooperation, and understanding. If just one of these legs is bent, broken, or mutilated, trust is impacted—or topples over completely. When all three legs are strong, however, trust is stable.

Trust is a stool with three legs: communication, cooperation, and understanding. GETTING TO WHY

Let's take a look at these three elements and see how they relate to trust as a whole.

Communication.

No other single element of humankind's capabilities has had more words and volumes written about it than communication. Yet in literally every company I have worked with in the past 30 years, communication is the number one area that everyone, from the custodial staff to the board members, wants to see improved.

However good people's intentions are, if they don't effectively communicate those intentions, then trust can't be established. I once worked with a CEO who would appear to be engaged in a conversation for about two minutes (unless he was the one doing the speaking). After those two minutes, he would jump on the phone to contact someone he had just thought about or check his email or look something up on the Internet or pull up a file to review. What was the message? You're not important. I'm done listening. I have better things to do.

We have recognized for many decades that communication has two major components: verbal and non-verbal. At best, the actual verbal component of your communication represents only about 40 percent of the total message. Hence, the majority of communication is non-verbal. Some of those non-verbal elements, like my CEO friend's behavior, can distort the message or send one that is antithetical to the communicator's purpose.

I warn clients that no matter how many ways you try to communicate a message—radio, television, email, blog post, newspaper, smoke signal, sky-writing, putting the message on both sides of people's checks—someone will say, "No one told me!" It is impossible to over-communicate.

Every parent has had a conversation with his or her child that featured the following exchange: "Yes I did." "No you didn't!" Another common version goes as follows: "No I didn't." "Yes you did!" I have also heard those words in every company I have worked with over the years. Just a different bunch of kids.

My CEO friend was setting himself up for a communication failure or at least a distortion. The bent communication leg on his stool of trust was telling people that they were not worth his time and attention and therefore not important to the company. Good employees have left companies for smaller slights than that. He was, in fact, a caring person who just wasn't—at that point—a good communicator. He agreed that there was room for improvement, and we made substantial progress in a short period of time.

I asked him to commit to multitasking-free conversations. The only activity that he could perform in a conversation other than listen was to take notes on what he was hearing. And speak occasionally. Not only did his listening skills improve but he finally began giving his employees the correct impression—that he genuinely cared.

Cooperation.

Cooperation is usually defined as working or literally "operating" together. The Japanese, however, have the wonderful concept of *wa*, which means harmony that allows the couple, family, company, or other organization to operate well.

The key point here is that trust is impossible without a willingness to work together on the part of the people involved. If the people around us don't *want* to have our back, then five will get you ten that they *won't* have our back when the crucial time comes. As a side note, I tell my clients that a simple assessment of leadership is to turn around and see who is following.

The enemies of such harmony are cynicism and selfishness, which organizations must battle constantly but gently. Acknowledging that there will be differing opinions and expectations while encouraging those differences to be shared or articulated is a sign of good management and leadership. I have met a lot of managers who say things like, "If I want your opinion, I'll give you one." Or, "If you were right, I would agree with you." Or how about, "Just sit down, shut up and get along." Needless to say, these statements are not good signs of cooperation being encouraged.

I worked with a company years ago that was having a disastrous day. The manufacturing plant of nearly 700 employees was having a line-down event, which means no product was being produced. I saw the plant manager, plant superintendent, supervisors, engineers, and other workers huddled around a large piece of equipment, poking and probing it every which way possible.

I asked one of the engineers what was up, and he replied that the lubricant that flowed through the overhead piping into the machine was not getting through. The machine was malfunctioning without this lubricant, and therefore the main production line was at a standstill. The company was losing thousands of dollars per hour because of this situation, and it had to be fixed immediately.

After learning what was going on, I noticed that one of the other supervisors I had been working with was standing about 30 feet from the machine, leaning against a post with his arms folded and a smile on his face. Virgil had been with the company for over 26 years and had been a supervisor in various departments for over 16 of those years.

I walked over to him and asked, "Do you know what's going on?"

"Sure," he said, "I saw this same thing happen about ten years ago."

"Do you know how to fix it?" I asked.

"Sure I do," he said, proceeding to tell me the process.

I then asked the million dollar question: "*Why* aren't you sharing this information with that frantic bunch of problem solvers over there?"

"I offered my help about 20 years ago," he said, "and they told me I wasn't an engineer or trained project manager, so I should just butt out. They can wallow in their mud for all I care."

"So you are not going to help or cooperate?" I asked.

"Nope, not unless they ask me to first," he said.

I walked over to the growing crowd of problem solvers and said to the chief engineer, "May I make a suggestion?" I then proceeded to convey the information that Virgil had just shared with me.

The engineer looked at me as though I had three eyes and a tail and said, "That's a great idea and insight. Where did you learn so much about this piece of equipment?"

I pointed to Virgil, who was still leaning against his post, and said, "He told me that you had the same problem about 10 years ago and that was how it was fixed."

The plant manager and vice president of operations both said at the same time, "*Why* didn't he tells us himself?"

"It's pretty simple," I said. "No one asked."

The problem was repaired in less than 30 minutes, and the plant was back in full operation.

In the distant past, management had shown an unwillingness to cooperate with Virgil, and he had been paying them back ever since with his own lack of cooperation. The result was a continual lack of trust on both sides.

Understanding.

Comprehending and correctly interpreting what others are saying is also essential to trust. "I just don't understand," is a comment I have heard thousands of times from parents, children, and managers who were expressing a lack of clarity about a situation, event, person, or thing. Even if communication is abundant and skillful and people have good intentions, a lack of understanding makes it all for naught, and trust is impossible.

In *Outliers: The Story of Success*, Malcolm Gladwell says that one of the major elements of motivation in today's workforces is having meaningful work, the kind that allows people to understand what their contribution is at the end of the day. Not having such an understanding can lead people to feel that their work serves no purpose, even if they are paid for their time, and they end up lacking the trust they need to be at their best.

One of the easiest places to see a lack or void of understanding is in marriage counseling, especially if it is centered on divorce or the potential of divorce. One of the partners says that something has changed and the relationship is no longer the same for him or her. The response comes: "I just don't understand." Or one of the partners says that a certain change is necessary for the relationship to remain viable. Again, "I just don't understand." The person on the side of change has a hard time explaining him- or herself, and the other partner has a hard time intuiting what is meant. Trust between the two will be broken until understanding is reestablished.

These same kind of exchanges are often heard in organizations and companies where change is wanted or needed, but people's lack of ability or willingness to understand the meaning and value of the change further compromises trust.

Three legs—one stool.

Since I was ten years old, my philosophy has been to trust people until they teach me not to do so. Someone can lose my trust by breaking off one of the legs of the stool. They can show an unwillingness to communicate, or they can communicate the wrong things. They can show an unwillingness to cooperate. Or they can show a complete lack of understanding of where I'm coming from, no matter how plainly I state my case.

Sometimes, however, I'll balance on two legs for awhile to give someone the chance to repair the third. In certain very rare cases, I have even hovered in the air on one leg for a brief period of time. When you understand how trust works, it's easy to be a little more forgiving.

Most people struggle with forgiveness. If you break a leg of the stool, trust is destroyed, and you're in trouble—in your marriage, your company, your church, or in any relationship or organization in which you're involved.

It's one of the tough facts of life that, once you're empowered with knowledge, the weight's on you to do the right thing, and trust is where this rule applies the most. I believe most people are looking for reasons to trust. Your job is to pick up the slack: communicate to the maximum degree possible, cooperate and foster cooperation to the maximum degree possible, and understand to the maximum degree possible.

People understand what you teach them. Teach them that trust is possible.

Please perform the exercise for this chapter in the workbook at the back of this book. The entire workbook may also be downloaded in PDF format for free at www.gettingtowhy.com.

Chapter Eighteen

Direction

Every organization—corporation, family, marriage, sports team, government—has a direction, even if it doesn't have a *Why*. As we pointed out at the very beginning of this book, *Why* is the fifth point of the compass: it orients you on the map of both the present and the future. An organization with a direction based on a strong *Why* understood by all is far more likely to be successful in its journey. An organization without this benefit is likely to find itself adrift at sea.

Part of getting to *Why* as a leader is managing direction. Right now, you are a leader of something. It may be the division of a corporation. It may be a small group at your church. You may be a co-leader in a relationship. At the very least, you are the leader of your own life and will need to communicate the direction of your life—the *Why* you have embraced—to others that are important to you.

Tough, firm, fair, consistent.

If you will recall, these were the qualities of your favorite teacher, who, of course, was an important leader in your life. Let's go through the qualities one by one to see how they relate to establishing and maintaining direction

Tough. A leader chooses a *Why* worth doing and communicates it to everyone in the organization. He or she makes sure that everyone understands that expectations are high and must be met. A leader also holds him- or herself to an equally high or higher standard and apologizes and makes amends when he or she fails to meet it.

Firm. A leader sticks to the same *Why* and never deviates from it without good reason. The mission is the mission.

Fair. A leader makes known to all their respective roles in fulfilling the mission, as well as the rewards of success and the consequences of failure. He or she plays by and judges according to the rules he or she has established and does not play favorites.

Consistent. A leader consistently pursues the goals and implements the processes he or she has established to fulfill the mission.

If a leader exemplifies these qualities, he or she has a very high probability of establishing and maintaining the successful direction of the organization. Yet there is one further condition for success in this task that challenges the abilities of even a word-class leader to the fullest.

Right now, you are a leader of something.

A leader constantly monitors and corrects the direction of the organization to keep it consistent with *Why*.

If I asked you to go on a long trip with me and told you we would probably be off course about 98% of the time, would you join me? Most people would simply say no.

Yet, during NASA's Apollo moon missions, the spacecraft was indeed off course 98% of the time, constantly pitching (rolling forward and backward) or yawing (rolling from side to side) or doing a combination of the two. Without constant monitoring and making corrections to these undesired conditions, the craft would be unable to reach the moon and bring its crew back alive.

Because of the Apollo missions, the word "telemetry" became known to millions of people. NASA developed an elaborate system that not only constantly measured and relayed the motion of the spacecraft but also activated tiny thruster rockets to return it to its proper position and course. At the same time, NASA was also monitoring the vital signs of the astronauts, as well as important capsule functions.

I remind companies and individuals that, like an Apollo mission, it's okay to be off course 98% of the time as long as you correct 100% of the time. Imagine you are traveling on a plane from Los Angeles to New York City in straight trajectory and are off course just one degree south the entire time. If you never get feedback on your location or correct your course, you will end up in Trenton, New Jersey—60 miles south of your intended destination. One degree is not much, but over time it destroys your objective.

For this reason, every organization requires a customized tracking system (remember the tracking we discussed in our chapter on goals? We're talking about the same thing here.). In other words, a scoreboard.

Establish a scoreboard and use it consistently.

When you happen upon a football game on TV, you want to know three things as soon as possible:

1. Who is playing?
2. What is the score?
3. How much time is left in the game?

Why is it we demand that information from our sports "telemetry" yet balk when asked to monitor performance in our work or personal development?

The issue that people have with scoreboards in work or personal life is that those tracking systems illuminate the dark corners where they are hiding and reveal how far off course they truly are. On the other hand, successful people celebrate scoreboards because they confirm the excellence of their performance and their contribution to the direction of the organization. They desire the light of measurement and tracking.

My dad once told me, "If I'm not yelling at you, then you're doing okay." This was a fairly primitive scoreboard, to say the least. Some managers and parents let their subordinates and children "pitch" and "yaw" willy-nilly, making corrections only when their charges are dramatically off course. This is very poor management and leadership. It is far better to establish a genuine tracking system, or scoreboard, so as to correct the course in real time and maintain that all-important direction.

Please perform the exercise for this chapter in the workbook at the back of this book. The entire workbook may also be downloaded in PDF format for free at www.gettingtowhy.com.

Chapter Nineteen

The Manager's Role

The manager's role is to *cause* the *right things* to be *done right* and *on time*.

The "right things" are the outputs that advance the organization in the right direction and help it realize its *Why*. Right things include everything from the actual products to production technology to accounting to janitorial services. An organization that does the right things is *effective*.

"Done right" means using as little in the way of resources as possible to create a given output: money, time, labor, raw materials, etc. An organization that does things right is *efficient*.

Efficiency, therefore, is much different from effectiveness. One of the problems we have in life is spending a lot of time and talent doing things right but discovering that it was the wrong thing. As *The One Minute Manager* author Ken Blanchard said, "Things not worth doing are not worth doing well."

"On time" means, of course, by the established deadline. I have trained thousands of managers and supervisors on this particular point, and again and again I have noted the tendency of people to assert that it's okay to deliver something late as long as it's "right." If work is late, however, then it hasn't been performed effectively and efficiently—it's been performed ineffectively and inefficiently. Be sure to close the escape route of lateness when you're in charge.

To sum up:

A manager is one who causes (by delegating) the

right things…	*effective*
to be done right…	*efficient*
on time.	*closes the escape route*

To "cause" is to delegate.

A manager causes the right things to be done right on time through *delegation*. A manager that doesn't delegate is just a worker with a nice title. We'll learn more about delegation in greater detail in an upcoming chapter.

A manager manages synergy, trust, and direction.

No matter how narrow or wide his or her particular area to manage, a manager works to increase synergy and trust while maintaining the direction of the team.

When delegating, a manager seeks to maximize the value of the team's "working together," or synergy. A manager whose teammates do not work well together either needs to manage better or rearrange the team.

When delegating, a manager seeks to maximize trust among the members of the team. A manager who harms trust by engaging in petty politics or other such practices is destroying value in the organization.

When delegating, a manager seeks to maintain the direction of the team and contribute to the maintenance of direction in the organization as a whole. A manager who delegates while causing the "wrong things" to be done is simply wasting the organization's resources.

The key to success as a manager.

My first three rules of management are…

1. Know your people.
2. Know your people.
3. Know your people.

The advanced course on management is…

1. Know your people better.

Sadly, one of the most consistent things I observe in managers is that they know very little about their people professionally and even less personally. Understanding a subordinate's or coworker's background and family situation can help create an extraordinarily healthy and trust-based culture for everyone. Seeking this understanding says clearly, "I'm interested in you, I care about what you do beyond work, and I care about how your situation impacts our work." On the other hand, when managers don't care, the effects are large and negative. People don't leave organizations; people leave people.

This is the "caring" we talked about in the chapter on creating a personal legacy. Those managers who care will seek to know their people. Those managers who seek to know their people will inevitably end up caring more.

Parents need to be great managers too: Know your kids. Know your kids. Know your kids. Parents need to be aware of distractions that can impact their kids' performance—not only as regards schoolwork but also social and family relationships.

Know your people.

The story of the cabinet company (knowing your people).

Many years ago, I was working with a large cabinet manufacturing company. I was out on the floor with the supervisor, and we were looking at one of the most complicated and sophisticated cutting machines they had in the facility. This monster cut pieces of wood in three different directions at the same time and could be very dangerous.

On a certain day, the machine operator was a man I happened to know personally from church. I turned to the supervisor and said, "You need to take him off this machine immediately."

The supervisor asked me that key question, "*Why*?"

"Did you not know that this man's wife is in the hospital? She had a heart attack three days ago," I said.

"No, I didn't know that," said the supervisor. "But *Why* should I take him off this machine?"

"This machine is very complicated," I said. "The operator must stay alert at all times to prevent a serious or even fatal accident. My concern is that he will be distracted by his wife's condition and lose focus."

"I appreciate that," said the supervisor, "but he's my best operator on that machine."

"That's even worse," I said. "Because he's so good on the machine, he could easily put himself on autopilot and create yet another opportunity for injury. The only other option I would suggest is to select a couple other people you'd like to train on this machine and have him begin training them. That way he would stay focused on the machine and the training, teaching his coworkers how to operate the machine safely and appropriately."

That is what we did. I also used this "teachable moment" to talk with the supervisor—who was a good guy overall—about the value of knowing one's people not just professionally but personally as well. Had this machine operator hurt himself on this occasion and the supervisor later found out about the wife's condition, the supervisor would have felt terrible.

Know your people. Care.

Please perform the exercise for this chapter in the workbook at the back of this book. The entire workbook may also be downloaded in PDF format for free at www.gettingtowhy.com.

CHAPTER TWENTY

THE DAO METHOD

I am confident that the DAO method is one of the most powerful tools in this book. If consistently applied, it can instantly increase a manager's overall success.

Conceptually, it's very simple. When a subordinate, partner, friend, or family member comes to you with a question, problem, etc., before saying anything else, ask, "Would you like my decision, advice, or opinion?" D, A, or O. You then respond appropriately.

A very high percentage of us are fixers. When our spouses, children, coworkers, subordinates, and so on come to us with a question, we are prone to come up with a decision on the spot—that is, to "fix" the situation. This is not always healthy for us, those asking the questions, or our organization. By using the DAO method, we respect the abilities of our subordinates and encourage them to be leaders in their own right.

Let's take a further look at the three choices we offer the questioner.

Decision. You tell the questioner what to do.

Advice. You coach the questioner on how to make his or her own decision. You might narrow down the options or specify a method for arriving at a decision.

Opinion. You simply serve as an expert or outside observer and lend your knowledge or experience. Often you simply comment on the options suggested by the questioner.

The following story illustrates the powerful transformation that using this method can effect.

The story of Jorge (using the DAO method).

Jorge was the director of a very large produce company that cut and packaged millions of dollars of fruit and vegetables each year. Jorge often told me how passionate he was about leadership and getting things done, which usually meant getting things done his way. I frequently observed people coming into Jorge's office and sharing a problem or asking a question, to which his immediate response was to offer his final decision on how to handle the matter at hand.

One day I said to Jorge, "You do know that people learn what you teach them, don't you?"

"What do you mean?" he said.

"You're teaching people that you have all the answers," I said.

"Is that a problem?" he asked.

"It certainly could be," I said. "If you handle all the problems and have all the answers, you're going to get all the problems. Quite frankly, many of these problems are a waste of your time and talent. Well beneath your pay grade. You're not taking advantage of the power of empowerment."

"I see," he said.

You're teaching people that you have all the answers.

GETTING TO WHY

"Some of the people who came into your office with questions and problems had already committed quite a bit of time to coming up with a solution, and they just wanted to share it with you. The decision they were looking for was the decision to support *their* decision. But you are consistently chopping their legs out from under them by not giving them the chance to share their thinking and problem-solving skills.

"So here's what I want you to do. The next time a person who comes into your office with a question or problem, ask if he or she is looking for a decision, advice, or opinion as early as possible in the conversation.

"If the person is looking for anything other than a decision, ask what his or her thinking has been thus far in the matter. Another thing I want you to work on is teaching your team that when they come to you with a question or problem, they can immediately ask for a decision, advice, or an opinion. I want your team to feel comfortable enough to say, 'I've already worked through a lot of this. I just need your input.'"

Jorge implemented the DAO method with great consistency, and over the next 30 days he learned quite a lot about his subordinates and his business.

Because he was asking them more questions about their thoughts on the issues they were sharing with him, Jorge realized he had several supervisors who were not good thinkers or decision-makers. He also learned he had some subordinates who were incapable of asking for advice or an opinion; all they wanted was a decision. On the other hand, he also learned who on his team were terrific decision-makers and leaders.

By repositioning himself as the advice- and opinion-giver, Jorge enhanced communication, cooperation, and understanding all at once, resulting in greater trust. He also was able to focus more attention on those employees who needed help in competencies and decision-making. The ultimate result was a significant improvement in performance and productivity.

Further, Jorge's supervisors also adopted the DAO method. They became more proud of their position, and their subordinates became more respectful of them. It was a very large and positive cultural shift throughout the organization.

There is an unfortunate epilogue to this story. Although Jorge was initially successful in implementing the DAO method, after about a month he began to backslide. His desire for control was simply too great, his personality overrode his good sense, and he once again disempowered his subordinates. Eventually, he was replaced, but the new manager, Don, implemented the DAO method with great success, and it remains an important part of the corporate culture.

I have met and coached hundreds of Jorges at all levels, both inside and outside the corporate world. It's especially satisfying to see the DAO method working with spouses or with parents and children. We stop becoming the fixers and start becoming the supporters, encouragers, and empowerers.

I remember a very emotional day when my daughter was completing a month of rehabilitation, and the patients were introducing their family and friends. She knew I was a fixer. In front of 200 people, she said, "Dad, you can't fix this one. I have to do it myself."

That's a tough thing for someone who specializes in counseling and consulting to hear—I knew way too much about her problem. But she was exactly right: I could not "fix this." I could not have been more proud of her at that moment.

When we give up the need to make all decisions, the temperature in the room changes. Shoulders relax. Moods shift. Empowerment is born.

Please perform the exercise for this chapter in the workbook at the back of this book. The entire workbook may also be downloaded in PDF format for free at www.gettingtowhy.com.

CHAPTER TWENTY-ONE

WIIFT? (WHAT'S IN IT FOR THEM?)

One of the oldest—and truest—motivational clichés I can remember is, "The more you help others get what they want, the more you'll get what you want." I've heard that statement in church, in Boy Scouts, in 4H, and from motivational speakers like Zig Ziglar.

My version of this cliché is, "What's in it for them?"—or WIIFT for short. It's important to understand that people act based on what *they* want, not what *we* want. When we sell, we must understand the needs of others and attempt to fulfill them with our products. When we manage, we must understand the needs of our subordinates and coworkers (part of "knowing your people") and motivate them based on what's important to them.

The concept with which more people are familiar is WIIFM—"What's in it for me?" We focused on this concept when we dealt with goals earlier in this book. A key point here, however, is that achieving success in our goals should not cost others their self-worth, self-esteem, self-respect, or goals. The skills of sharing *Why* are similar to putting together a puzzle. You must continually look how the pieces—what's in it for me, what's in it for them—create the desired picture.

The following two stories illustrate the right way and the wrong way to approach the issue.

The story of Jack (not understanding WIIFT).

Jack was the president of a very large and very rapidly growing company that in less than three years had acquired seven or eight businesses. Jack's empire was ranked the fastest growing company in the state for three consecutive years, in one year logging 1,200% year-over-year growth. What I first noticed about this CEO and would-be leader was that the pronoun "I" dominated his speech:

"I did."

"I have."

"I want."

"I will."

Jack prided himself on a management technique he himself called (no joking here) "Management by Intimidation." He had no concern for others; WIIFT never went anywhere near his brain cells. I tried explaining to him that his type of management style generally resulted in one of two things: having people around him that he could manipulate and be servants to him, or having people who would want to punch him in the nose and work for somebody else with better pronouns.

Jack prided himself on a management technique he himself called "Management by Intimidation."

GETTING TO WHY

I sadly watched Jack's publicly traded company go from $12.00 per share in value to $0.10 per share in a spectacularly short period of time.

Jack had built his dominion through acquisitions and financial leverage, but was completely unable to hang onto competent people. I watched highly educated, highly skilled people walk out the door while a retinue of incompetent yes-men and yes-women remained. The company became both ineffective and inefficient in delivering its products, and it was eaten alive by the competition.

Jack never acknowledged his failure—at least not while I was around. He blamed his subordinates, market forces, government regulators—anyone but himself. He left behind a sad legacy of several companies acquired and destroyed and many lives negatively affected.

The story of Carl (understanding WIIFT).

My friend Carl is the world's biggest extrovert and a fantastic salesperson. He loves being around people, gathering new relationships by the carload, and growing his contact list to the maximum.

Carl prides himself on learning something special about a person and buying him or her a small but thoughtful gift based on that information.

One day, I accompanied Carl as he called on a potential client. Carl had learned that the director of human resources was a fanatical Butler University basketball fan and alumnus. As we sat down with him to discuss business, Carl pulled out a large photograph of a basketball game in progress at the famous Hinkle Fieldhouse. The HR director lit up like a Roman candle. He and Carl spent the next 20 minutes discussing the picture and Butler University. Carl walked away with a new friend and a new relationship and the knowledge that he had made someone else happy. The only problem was that we didn't end up discussing business much, and Carl didn't get the deal.

I asked Carl at what point was he going to present his services to the HR director. He said, "Oh, we'll reschedule that."

"Carl, you're a professional visitor, not a salesperson. You could, however, be very successful if you could use your incredible people skills to connect your product with clients' needs."

Ultimately, Carl and I worked together to refocus and reshape his storytelling skills into a very successful career in public speaking. He loves doing research and converting what he learns into powerful presentations. His product now connects WIIFM and WIIFT in a powerful way.

Go beyond manipulation to genuine caring.

The story of Jack illustrates not caring about WIIFT at all, whereas the story of Carl illustrates caring with a genuinely good heart. A third approach, used by crafty people in all eras and places, is to understand people's needs and motivations and use them to manipulate.

Needless to say, that is not my recommendation. People who build good and powerful legacies use the concept of WIIFT to help people be happy and make the world a little better. Also, in my experience, using WIIFT with altruistic intentions is much more likely to produce success than using it without. As in most things in life, genuine caring wins the day.

Please perform the exercise for this chapter in the workbook at the back of this book. The entire workbook may also be downloaded in PDF format for free at www.gettingtowhy.com.

Chapter Twenty-Two

Delegation

As I said in the chapter on the role of the manager, a manager causes things to happen by delegation. Managers who do not delegate are not managers at all, but merely workers with the particular rank of "manager" or "supervisor."

Moreover, when a manager does not delegate, the message he or she is sending very often is, "I don't trust you." When I share this insight with leaders and managers, however, they are almost always surprised or shocked.

Consider this, however: Do you ever remember watching a parent or supervisor do a task you could do and asking him or her, "*Why* didn't you ask me to do that? What's the matter—don't you trust me?"

The person probably denied it was an issue of trust and had a nominally valid reason *Why* he or she didn't delegate: "I knew you were busy." "It would have taken more time to teach you how to do it." And so on.

When we don't delegate, it's not our intent to tell people we don't trust them; it's simply the result. We need to avoid sending that message.

On the other hand, when we are asked to help with or take over a task or responsibility, we immediately feel more valued, honored, and trusted. Delegating helps others feel this way, empowering them to participate in fulfilling the mission.

When managers choose not to delegate, more is at stake than the effectiveness and efficiency of the company. The motivation of his or her subordinates is also hanging in the balance.

Eliminate, simplify, delegate, do.

When it comes to delegation, we need to consider the above four options at all times.

Eliminate those tasks that are not "right things."

Simplify tasks. Eliminate any part of a task that is not a "right thing."

Delegate tasks, either wholly or partially. Never assume that a task that has been performed by one person until now must be performed that way forever.

Do tasks yourself when that is truly the most efficient way.

The steps of delegation.

Once the above is understood, delegation becomes a simpler concept and easier to perform. The following are the steps of delegation:

1. Choose the right person or team for a task so as to maximize effectiveness, efficiency, and synergy.
2. Establish and explain the level of delegation. Inform the delegatee of the Delegatee's Bill of Rights (explained below).
3. Establish tough but fair expectations of the person or team so as to establish direction.
4. Train the person or team to perform the task, or delegate the training. Provide the person or team the tools and equipment needed to perform the task.
5. Monitor the person's performance with a scoreboard and provide regular feedback to maintain direction (not a generic yearly review!).

Sounds simple, doesn't it? It's the essence of management, yet I have met thousands of "supervisors" who were not implementing any of the five steps.

The two big pitfalls of delegation.

One of the big pitfalls in delegation is the assumption on the part of the delegator that the delegatee will perform all of his or tasks at exactly the level of autonomy that the delegator desires. The second big pitfall in delegation is the assumption on the part of the delagatee that all tasks are to be performed at a level of autonomy with which he or she is comfortable or familiar. Without setting clear expectations, problems are virtually inevitable.

For example, Jane is the supervisor and delegator and Sarah is Jane's assistant and the delegatee. For the past year, Sarah has been answering the phone and filing papers with a very high level of autonomy. She performs these tasks and informally reports to Jane as needed. She also receives client queries from Jane to answer, and she always receives confirmation from Jane before emailing the replies. Sarah is performing this latter task at a lower level of autonomy, but the two women have never spoken explicitly about such levels; in fact, they have never even thought about it.

One day Jane decides to delegate a new task to Sarah: managing Jane's appointments. Sarah is familiar with the calendar software, since she uses it for her own appointments. There is no training or talk about a level of delegation.

Here is where our two pitfalls come into play. Let's consider two scenarios.

Scenario 1. Since Sarah is already answering the phone for Jane, she starts making appointments for her when people call. She does what she thinks is reasonable, setting up appointments with important clients at times she's pretty sure that Jane will find acceptable. Sarah unconsciously assumes that the level of autonomy for the new task is the same as that for the task of answering the phone. Returning from a business trip, Jane is appalled that Sarah has made numerous appointments for her without checking with her first.

Scenario 2. Sarah answers the phones, and several clients mention wanting to meet with Jane. Sarah takes a note for each one but does not book any meetings. She assumes that the level of delegation for the new task is the same as for the task of answering client queries. Returning from a business trip, Jane is appalled that Sarah has not been more proactive in getting things on the calendar.

Far from unrealistic, problems like these are daily occurrences in organizations everywhere. Establishing the level of delegation when a task is assigned, however, has the power to eliminate such problems entirely.

The levels of delegation.

The following are the levels of delegation. It forms a very effective system with the steps of delegation and the Delegatee's Bill of Rights. Here are the levels with explanations for each.

1. **Don't do anything until I tell you.**
   At first glance this might not seem to be delegation at all, since the delegatee is being guided or monitored throughout the performance of the task. Nevertheless, delegation at this level establishes who will be performing the task. Further, per the Delegatee's Bill of Rights, you will be making clear many other things as well, such as deadlines, performance expectations, training steps, etc. Often Level 1 is used during a training or acclimation period, after which the level is increased.

2. **Check with me before you do it. Report back right after you do it.**
   The difference with Level 1 is that the delegatee is not guided or monitored at all times. The delegator wants to confirm the delegatee's understanding of the proper approach to the task before it is performed and confirm proper execution and/or results immediately afterward.

3. **Check with me before you do it. Report back routinely (daily, weekly, monthly).**
   The delegator wants to confirm the delegatee's understanding of the proper approach to the task before it is performed but does not need immediate confirmation of proper execution and/or results afterward.

4. **Do it. Report back right after you do it.**
   The delegator does not need to confirm the delegatee's understanding of the approach to the task. Perhaps the delegatee is sufficiently skilled or the task is completely routine. Nevertheless, the delegator wants to confirm proper execution and/or results afterward.

5. **Do it. Report back routinely (daily, weekly, monthly).**
   This is the highest level of autonomy. The delegator does not need to confirm anything with the delegatee before or immediately after the task is performed. Nevertheless, there is always a need to report back at some point, since there must *always* be a system in place to track performance and results for each task.

Once you put them into practice a bit, you'll find that these levels become second nature to you and the members of your team.

The Delegatee's Bill of Rights.

Over the years, I have developed the following "Delegatee's Bill of Rights" to prevent inept and unfair delegation. Each of the rights is not only something that delegatees desire but also something that prevents delegation from failing.

THE DELEGATEE'S BILL OF RIGHTS

For every task delegated, a delgatee has the right to know and provide his or her opinion on the following:

1. What the task and deadline are.
2. What level of task quality and performance is expected, how quality and performance will be measured and tracked, and how and when feedback will be provided.
3. *Why* the task is being delegated to him or her and not someone else.
4. What the benefits of delegation are for both the delegator and the delegatee.
5. How the task ranks in priority compared to other tasks for which the delegatee is responsible.
6. Whether one or more of the delegatee's current tasks can be delegated to others so that the delegatee can focus on the new task.
7. Who is going to train the delegatee and what are the steps of that training. What are the tools needed (computer, production equipment, or anything needed to perform the task), an dwho will provide the training on them.

As the delegator, you should not passively inform the delegatee of these rights and ask, "Any questions?" Rather, you should proactively go over each of these rights with the delegatee at the time of delegation. They are as much for your benefit as for his or hers. The Getting to *Why* Delegation Worksheet included in the workbook lays out the entire process out for you.

What are we trying to prevent with the above rights? Here are the reasons (*Whys*) for each in the same order:

1. Discussing what the task and deadline are establishes the fundamentals of the job (you'd be surprised how something so basic is often ignored!).

2. Discussing what level of task quality and performance is expected, how quality and performance will be measured and tracked, and how and when feedback will be provided confirms that the task is measurable and trackable and allows the delegatee to prepare for the measuring and tracking systems.
3. Discussing *Why* the task is being delegated to the delegatee and not someone else makes clear to the delegatee that the job is not being imposed unfairly upon him or her. Making the *Why* of delegation clear is essential to maintaining trust.
4. Discussing what the benefits of delegation are for both the delegator and the delegatee ensures that WIIFM and WIIFT is understood by both sides. Too often we delegate while failing to create a motivational environment and maintain trust.
5. Discussing how the task ranks in priority compared to other tasks helps maintain direction. Not all jobs that we delegate are of first importance, and some are delegated strictly on a "when you have time" basis. We need to keep priorities clear from the start.
6. Discussing whether one or more of the delegatee's current tasks can be delegated to others respects the delegatee's own ideas for delegation and help him or her be as efficient as possible.
7. Discussing who is going to train the delegatee and what the steps of that training will be ensures that training is considered from the beginning of the process. Moreover, making clear what tools are needed from the beginning helps ensure that they will provided in a timely manner. All too often it is assumed that training will simply "happen." Without proper planning, it almost never does.

By implementing this Bill of Rights in your organization firmly and consistently, you will see amazing results. It can be implemented in families just as successfully as in corporations.

The main reasons *Why* delegatees resist delegation.

People will sometimes not want to do a task that you would like to delegate to them. Sometimes their resistance is due to a genuine dislike of the particular task. By all means, if there is someone else to do it more enthusiastically (and therefore perhaps better), then a good manager will choose that person. If, however, there is no one more appropriate for the task, then the manager will need to be firm in his or her request to the original delegatee.

A more common reason for resistance, however, is a fear of failure on the part of the delegatee. The Delegatee's Bill of Rights exists in part to alleviate this fear by allowing the delegatee to provide feedback during the delegation process and learn how he or she will be trained. If, during the process, it comes out that the delegatee is insecure about his or her prospects for success, then the manager can consider whether these fears are justified and take appropriate measures.

Delegation is not abdication.

The worst type of manager is one who assigns a task to a subordinate without adequate planning or training and avoids responsibility for the results when they are poor. This is not delegation; this is abdication.

A manager is always responsible for the results of his or her subordinates' performance. If a manager discovers along the way that the subordinate is unequal to the task or that the task output is not a "right thing," then he or she needs to take corrective measures, going to his or her own superior for help if necessary.

The story of George (the power of delegation).

Years ago, I was training 15 supervisors at a manufacturing plant in East Central Indiana. George was the head of maintenance for the plant and was behind in at least a dozen projects—some for more than two years.

The problem was that George would not delegate to his three subordinates. As a way of helping George without singling him out, I asked the 15 supervisors to write down and share with the group one or two tasks that they were currently performing but hated to do.

When it was George's turn to share, he said, "I really, really hate inspecting the dozens and dozens of fire extinguishers in the plant all the time, but OSHA requires it."

After everyone had shared his or her most dreaded task, I handed out a sheet similar to the Getting to *Why* Delegation Worksheet and asked them to put their most hated task at the top of the page. I then told them that they had one week to take that task off their to-do list and delegate it to a subordinate.

I thought George was going to have a heart attack. He immediately began wailing, "Everybody knows how much I hate those darn fire extinguishers. If I give this task to someone, they're going to think I'm dumping on them."

I looked at George and smiled, saying, "I don't care, George. You have one week." The group applauded, anticipating George's future "fun" in delegating the task.

One week later, as I began the training, I noticed George leaning back in his chair, smiling and whistling. I had to ask: "What's up, George?"

George would not delegate to his three subordinates.

"It took me five days to get up the courage to delegate the fire extinguisher task," he said. "When I selected Michael and asked him if he'd do it, he lit up and said, 'Absolutely! We all know how much you hate that task; I'll be glad to take it off your hands!' He then created a log book, which he carries with him all the time, and he doesn't pass a fire extinguisher without checking it and making sure it's up to spec. Michael has become the fire marshal of our plant."

"So *Why* are you smiling, George?" I asked. "Is that it?"

"That went so well," said George, "that I ended up delegating three other tasks."

I said to George and the group, "What does this show us? That you're only delegating a task—not your attitude about the task. As you can see, Michael did not have the same attitude about the task that George did. Your delegatees will similarly have their own attitudes toward tasks you give to them."

Within 90 days, George ended up completing more than half of his project list. He was able to focus his talent where it belonged: managing the big picture of plant maintenance.

Guide to the Getting to *Why* Delegation Planning Worksheet.

(The worksheet is located in the workbook at the back of this book.)

The Delegation Planning Worksheet takes you through the steps of the "Delegatee's Bill of Rights" that I provided in the previous chapter. Like the Getting to *Why* Goal Planning Worksheet, this worksheet is intended to be scribbled upon and thoroughly discussed by delegatee and delegator. Feel free to use separate sheets of paper as needed.

Let's go through the steps one by one. Keep in mind that the delegatee should be able to provide his or her opinion at each stage.

1A. Task. This is a brief description of the task sufficient to identify it.

1B. Deadline. The task may have a one-time deadline or a recurring deadline, such as once a month.

2A. Quality and Performance Expectations/Measurements. Here is where you write down such basic expectations as sales quotas, amount of work done per hour, and so on. Qualitative expectations are also appropriate: "Great customer service," etc.

2B. Quality and Pperformance Tracking System. The system you will use to track the expectations/measurements you noted in 2A above.

2C. Feedback Provider(s). The people who will provide feedback to the delegatee about task performance.

2D. Feedback Date(s). This can be a one-time review about a completed task or a recurring performance review. I suggest providing feedback early and often. A generic, half-hearted "yearly review" is not acceptable!

3. Reason for Choosing Delegatee. The delegatee needs to know that he or she was chosen for appropriate reasons. It's important to confirm that the choice of delegatee was the best possible under current circumstances.

4. Benefits to Delegatee/Delegator. Filling this out helps the delegator confirm that the delegatee will be motivated to perform the task. At the same time, doing so helps motivate the delegatee while explaining the intentions of the delegator.

5. Task Priority and Delegation Level. Filling this section out provides considerable illumination as to how the new task relates to current tasks. The delegatee's current tasks should be ranked 1-5 in the "Priority rank" column, with "1" for the most important task and "5" for the least important task. The delegation level for each task should also be entered in the "Delegation Level" column.

6. Can This Task be Delegated? Now it's time to review whether the delegatee's current tasks should in turn be delegated so that the delegatee can focus on the new task. Of course, you should also consider simplifying or eliminating these tasks as well.

7. Training and Tools Plan. Here is a place to enter the training steps, tools, trainers, target dates for training step completion, and the dates on which steps are actually completed. If training is not required for a particular tool, simply put "N/A" in the "Trainer" column. "Target Date" refers to when the training step ought to be completed or the tool provided. "Date Completed/Provided" refers to when the training step is actually completed or the tool actually provided.

Guide to the Getting to *Why* Delegation Planning Worksheet Reference Sheet.

The first time you fill out a Delegation Planning Worksheet with a subordinate, please go over the Reference Sheet with him or her first. You should both sign and date it, and you should retain a copy of the page to confirm that you have reviewed the Delegatee's Bill of Rights and the levels of delegation together. The subordinate can then refer to the sheet as necessary going forward.

It's important to keep in mind that delegating is not limited to entrusting tasks to others that you yourself are currently performing. It may be a task that a subordinate or colleague is performing, that someone in another department is performing, or that no one in the company has ever performed. In every such case, you should fill out a delegation worksheet.

After the sheet is filled out, copies should be made for every person involved: delegator, delegatee, trainers, etc., and they should of course be directed to file their sheets and review them at appropriate intervals. As manager, you should keep all of your delegation sheets for all employees in an orderly filing system and review them regularly.

Finally, there is a second sheet that both the delegator and delegatee should read through completely, discuss, sign, and date the first time the delegator delegates a task to the delegatee. This sheet includes the levels of delegation and Delegatee's Bill of Rights, and it should be kept by the delegatee for future reference.

Simply by using the Getting to *Why* Delegation Planning Worksheet, you have made yourself a better delegator than the vast majority of managers. It is a powerful tool that makes work much easier and more productive for both you as manager and your subordinates.

Please perform the exercise for this chapter in the workbook at the back of this book. The entire workbook may also be downloaded in PDF format for free at www.gettingtowhy.com.

Chapter Twenty-Three

Succession Planning

Succession planning is the ultimate form of delegation: you delegate everything you do to one or more people and move up in the organization—or leave completely. In either case, you are moving on to a new Self and a new Why.

I'm a firm believer that succession planning should be done everywhere in the organization, from CEO to custodian. Far too often, however, companies wait until a position is empty and take rushed, less effective measures to fill it.

I've helped many companies perform succession planning, and often I've had to make top executives aware that such a thing even exists. When I've asked, "Who would take your place if you were to be promoted?" far too often I've received the answer, "I don't have anyone to take my place."

When I hear that, I'm tempted to ask, "Is that because you're so insecure that you haven't trained someone to do your job? Or are you so arrogant that you didn't think any subordinate could do your job? Or do you manage your time so poorly that you just didn't get around to it?" I bite my tongue, since I know that, in most cases, the manager has simply never even considered the matter.

Often managers sabotage their own careers by not doing succession planning: since there is no one to replace them, they themselves cannot rise to a higher position.

For years I have taught managers and leaders that one of the best compliments in the world of business comes from a subordinate who says, "I want your job, and I still want you to be my boss." The person may very well be ready and able to push you up—not out—to greater success. I challenge you to create that kind of culture.

Succession planning is the ultimate form of delegation.

GETTING TO WHY

The method of effective succession planning.

The first step of succession planning is to lay out all of the tasks for which a person is responsible—not just the ones that are usually thought of as going with his or her position. For example, if the CFO is also running projections for marketing, then that task needs to have its own delegation plan. It can't be assumed that anyone applying for the CFO position will also be able to perform marketing work. In addition, although it sounds obvious, it should be verified that the candidate is aware of and capable of performing each task in the job description.

Once each of the tasks a person performs is identified and described, you create a delegation worksheet for each. Consider that some tasks can be eliminated completely. Further, you may discover that certain tasks can and should be delegated immediately to others instead of waiting for the successor. In addition, it may be discovered that, in the future, not all of the tasks should go to one person, or even a person in the same department. This set of delegation worksheets is an excellent kind of job description. Usually, you will not need to create more than ten worksheets for a position.

Next, you identify the person who will succeed to the set of tasks. You go over the delegation sheets and the Delegatee's Bill of Rights for each and every task, confirming that the candidate is appropriate and establishing the training that he or she will require.

Finally, you begin the training process, keeping track of progress and providing feedback to the successor. During the process, be ready to correct your course: the candidate may require additional training than what was originally planned, and in some cases a candidate may prove inadequate and not a viable candidate at all.

To recap the steps:

1. Identify all of the tasks the current executive or employee performs.
2. Create delegation worksheets for each task. Combine the delegation worksheets into one set (job description), separating out those tasks that are best delegated elsewhere.
3. Identify a candidate to succeed to the task set.
4. Go over the tasks with the candidate, carefully and consistently covering the Delegatee's Bill of Rights for each.
5. Train the candidate, as necessary, to take on the tasks.
6. Continuously monitor the candidate's progress, taking measures as necessary to correct the course.

To be effective, succession planning requires a kind of apprenticeship in which *Why* is shared and passed on. Successors to senior and upper level management positions usually require a minimum of two to five years of special training.

Using this method for self-succession planning.

The method is the same, except you will create two delegation worksheet sets: one for the old you, and one for the new you.

For the old you, you will go through the above method, delegating to others as necessary. You will make sure that you can leave your old *Why*, Self, and life as smoothly as possible.

For the new you, you will also create a delegation worksheet set, imagining that your future self is handing it to you. Based on your goal worksheets, you'll identify all the tasks that the new you will take on, confirm your ability to perform them, and arrange for training as necessary. Even though you are delegating these tasks to yourself, you will rigorously go through the Delegatee's Bill of Rights for each.

Perform succession planning for the organization of the future.

Succession planning is all about the future; it is therefore performed for the organization of the future, not the present. To fill its ranks effectively, the organization needs to get to *Why* and establish long-term goals.

Great succession planning requires a finger constantly on the pulse of the organization. Someone must be aware of current needs while attempting to predict future needs. If the CEO or leader can't do this, he or she needs to find someone who can.

A company should nurture future managers so that they are prepared for the time that they will likely succeed to their new position. The candidates should therefore be intimately familiar with the company's long-term strategy and its various financial and marketing projections.

Identifying appropriate candidates.

Needless to say, the more difficult the group of tasks that a person handles, the more difficult it is to find his or her successor. C-level executives are notoriously difficult to replace, and that's one reason *Why* training their successors takes so long. Above and beyond confirming that the candidate can perform the tasks of the job, you need to assess more abstract qualities, such as the candidate's character, potential as a leader, and fit with the organization's culture.

Thus, appropriate candidates for high-level positions are generally those who have gone up through the ranks and exhibited excellent performance and judgment, regardless of the specific positions they've occupied. In almost every case, great candidates respect others and are respected by others in the organization. They don't perceive present or future positions as an entitlement but instead as an honor.

On the other hand, candidates that look good on paper don't always work out in real life. One must always have a Plan B.

The story of Gus (ineffective succession planning).

Gus ran one of the largest furniture chains in Indiana, which had been founded by his father. Gus had had a long, successful career but never named, much less trained, a successor. On the board of directors sat eight other members of his family. When Gus retired, the board had an even number of people and was thus often split evenly when it came time to vote.

I was asked to work with them on some organizational planning and development. One of the first things I asked them was, "Who is going to become the president and leader of the company?" I looked around the table, and not one single person could or would answer me. So I then asked, "Who wants to be president?" Four people answered in the affirmative, and chaos ensued.

Each of them was certain he deserved the position, citing such reasons as number of years in the company, current job title, and relationship to Gus. (Gus's son was one of the four, yet he was also the youngest and least experienced among them.)

This group and I met at 6:00 a.m. on four consecutive Tuesday mornings until one morning I literally jumped up on the conference table and yelled at them, "You guys are killing this company! You are each afraid that someone else is going to have more power, authority, responsibility, or recognition than you. Your only interest is in making sure that doesn't happen. I don't care if you guys take turns every month, every week, or even every day, but someone has to sit in the CEO's chair and make decisions for the company, with the rest cooperating. If you can't do that, then sell the company because you're going to go bankrupt."

Having said that, I jumped off the table, turned to them and said, "Today, I'm firing you!" and walked out. Six months later they sold the company to a major national furniture chain, and two of the board members came to work for me.

This company had not performed succession planning at all, much less effectively, but at least the board members had the wisdom to sell out and preserve the value that the company contained.

The story of the bakery (effective succession planning).

This story is another that demonstrates the need for effective succession planning. I was doing consulting for one of the largest bakeries in the country, and the founder and his son and nephew were its key leaders. The founder had created relationships with other baking companies and was poised to make his company one of the strongest bakeries in the world. Yet he died suddenly in his late fifties.

The son and nephew took over the company as co-presidents for a while and tried to make a go of it, but the relationships the founder had created disappeared, and the company simply didn't have the funds to support two highly compensated CEOs.

So one day the cousins sat down to decide who would be president, since clearly their current system was not working. Two hours later, they shook hands, and the nephew of the prior owner became the president of the company—not the son.

The son supported his cousin, recognizing his skills and abilities, and began looking for a new career. That company is now in its fourth generation and doing better than ever. What the founder did right was nurturing two managers capable of taking his place. His only mistake was not having an explicit plan in place to cover the eventuality of his own death. Fortunately, however, his son and nephew were of excellent character and resolved the issue like gentlemen and professionals.

Please perform the exercise for this chapter in the workbook at the back of this book. The entire workbook may also be downloaded in PDF format for free at www.gettingtowhy.com.

Epilogue

Congratulations, you have asked and by now have probably answered or gone a long way toward answering the ultimate question: *Why?* In doing so, you have joined a group that makes up only a small percentage of the total population. Most people never ask the question in the first place or ask it only when it is safe to ask. You've gone beyond what is safe and secure to take a risk, for asking *Why* is always a risk.

I have downloaded over 40 years' worth of experiences, mistakes, knowledge, and—I hope—wisdom into this book. I also hope it has been helpful, encouraging, and meaningful to you.

I am very conscious of the supporting characters of *Why*, and they may have entered your mind from time to time as you read this book:

- ***How* do I get to my destination?** *How* is the method question, letting us engage in best practices in everything we do.
- ***What* do I do next?** *What* is the selector question, allowing us to narrow down a virtually infinite set of options.
- ***Which* of my options do I choose?** *Which* is the discriminator question, allowing us to pick from our options after we have narrowed them down.
- ***When* do I begin?** *When* is the time management question, helping us deal with the ultimate "limited resource."
- ***Where* do I do fulfill my mission?** *Where* is the locator question, helping us choose the best places for all of our activities.
- ***Who* should go with me?** *Who* is the relationship question, helping us choose the best people for our lives and our goals.
- ***If* I succeed, then what do I do?** *If* is the possibility question, helping us see beyond our current horizon.

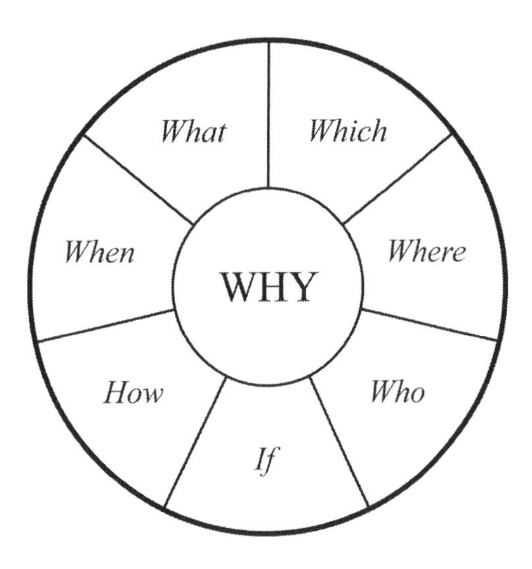

Do you notice the resemblance with the graphic in the chapter on the Areas of Life? It's no coincidence. Just as *you* are at the core of your life, surrounded by the Seven Areas, *Why* is the core question of life, surrounded by the other seven questions.

Life is a contact sport: the more people, places, and things with which you come in contact, the more you find fulfillment. Going forward, I will write more about the questions above to help readers achieve even better "contact" in life. In the meantime, feel free to visit my website—www.leadtogreat.com—or email me with your questions and comments: jb@leadtogreat.com. I wish you peace and wellness.

—JB Symons

About the Authors

JB Symons

JB is the president of Lead to Great, a leadership and organizational consulting group that helps people in organizations of all types and sizes play better together. He grew up on a farm near Muncie, Indiana, and began working at age eight. Serving three tours of duty in Vietnam as a corpsman on assignments with the Navy Seals Teams, he saw the worst that man can do to man. Over the years, JB has been a farmer, pastor, therapist, family counselor, bartender, folksinger, salesman, business owner, professor, husband, and father.

JB started the first of several successful businesses in 1975 and has learned firsthand the challenges and rewards of running a company in various economic climates. For over 35 years, he has shared his know-how and insights with hundreds of companies and businesses, from small one-person offices to Fortune 500 corporations. With degrees in biology, divinity, and psychology, JB has a passion for developing healthy people and corporate environments. He lives in Indianapolis, Indiana, and relaxes in Austin, Texas.

Matt Rouge

Born in Indianapolis, Matt became interested in writing and Asian cultures in high school. After graduating from Loyola University in Chicago, Matt lived for eight years in Japan, becoming fluent in the language and culture and working as an English teacher, trading company salesman, and marketing manager in the drug and semiconductor industries.

With a Master of Science in Management from Purdue and extensive experience in the marketing field, Matt translates and writes advertising copy and PR for some of the world's largest companies, including major automakers. Eleven of Matt's short stories have been published in high-circulation print magazines, and four of his plays have been produced in community theater in his second home, New York City.

GETTING TO *WHY*
Workbook

Including exercises for every chapter in the book
by
JB Symons with Matt Rouge

Name: ____

Co./org.: ____

Date begun: ____

Date completed: _____________________________________

Notes: ____

____

Download this workbook for free at **www.gettingtowhy.com**

Before you begin…

The following exercises are simple but powerful, revealing to you the life you wish to live and your current position in it. Answer as honestly and frankly as you can: only you will write, read, and ponder your answers, but getting them down on paper can have a surprisingly big effect on your understanding of your life and yourself.

In fact, I have learned through years of experience that writing down thoughts—even if they seem negative or superficial or embarrassing or otherwise undesirable—is a key part of attaining personal change. Just answering in your head doesn't cut it—trust me! So please write down your answers. Use additional sheets of paper or type up your answers if you desire. You'll reap big rewards in understanding yourself.

You may respond to these questions either personally or professionally or both. The more you can reveal about yourself, the more you will see.

GETTING TO *WHY*

Exercise for Chapter 1: Why ***Why****?*

1. In what I am doing now, what is giving me the greatest sense of accomplishment?

The least sense of accomplishment?

2. What are my top five personal strengths?

1.

2.

3.

4.

5.

Top five personal weaknesses?

1.

2.

3.

4.

5.

3. What do people praise me for most often?

Criticize me for most often?

____

____

____

4. What have I done to improve myself in the last twelve months?

____

____

____

5. Do I have a secret project or private plan for "sometime" in life? If so, what is it?

____

____

____

6. If at some time in the future a statue were created in my honor, I would want its plaque to list the following things I will have accomplished.

____

____

____

7. As a result of reviewing what I've written above, what are my top five motivators?
(Examples: *recognition, acceptance, money, power, prestige, status in company, love of family, etc.*)

1. ____

2. ____

3. ____

4. ____

5. ____

GETTING TO *WHY*

Exercise for Chapter 2: Pleasure and Satisfaction

1. What are the Top 5 things giving me pleasure in life right now?

1. ______________________________

2. ______________________________

3. ______________________________

4. ______________________________

5. ______________________________

2. What are the Top 5 things giving me pain in life right now?

1. ______________________________

2. ______________________________

3. ______________________________

4. ______________________________

5. ______________________________

3. What is my overall level of satisfaction and dissatisfaction with my life as a whole right now?

____

____

____

4. Based on my answers above, where would I place myself on the Pain-Pleasure, Satisfaction-Dissatisfaction Graph?

____

____

____

5. *Why* am I located where I am on the graph?

____

____

____

Exercise for Chapter 3: Success and Failure

1. What are my Top 5 successes in life thus far?

1. ____________________
2. ____________________
3. ____________________
4. ____________________
5. ____________________

2. What are my Top 5 failures in life thus far?

1. ____________________
2. ____________________
3. ____________________
4. ____________________
5. ____________________

3. Who are the Top 5 people in my life supporting my success?

1. ____________________
2. ____________________
3. ____________________
4. ____________________
5. ____________________

4. Who are the people close to me who do not support my success?

____

____

5. Who are the people close to me whose success I do not support?

____

____

6. Going forward, what is my definition of success for myself?

____

____

GETTING TO *WHY*

Exercise for Chapter 4: The Seven Areas of Life

In this exercise, you will rate your level of pleasure/pain and satisfaction/dissatisfaction in each of your Seven Areas of Life. The ratings are as follows:

5: Maximal pleasure/satisfaction
4: Intense pleasure/satisfaction
3: Considerable pleasure/satisfaction
2: Moderate pleasure/satisfaction
1: Mild pleasure/satisfaction
0: Neutral/can't tell
-1: Mild pain/dissatisfaction
-2: Moderate pain/dissatisfaction
-3: Considerable pain/dissatisfaction
-4: Intense pain/dissatisfaction
-5: Maximal pain/dissatisfaction

Please score your current level of pleasure (P) and satisfaction (S) in each area by putting a check mark in the appropriate boxes.

		-5	-4	-3	-2	-1	0	1	2	3	4	5
Physical and Health	P											
	S											
Mental and Educational	P											
	S											
Spiritual	P											
	S											
Social	P											
	S											
Family and Home	P											
	S											
Financial	P											
	S											
Career	P											
	S											

In what quadrant am I located in each of the Seven Areas of Life? *Why* did I score myself as I did?

Physical and Health

Mental and Educational

Spiritual

Social

Family and Home

Financial

Career

GETTING TO *WHY*

Exercise for Chapter 5: Avoiding the Role Trap

For each of the Seven Areas of Life, consider whether there are any roles in which you find yourself currently trapped. If so, describe the role, how you assess yourself positively or negatively, and ***Why*** you are currently trapped.

The Roles in Which I Am Currently Trapped

Physical and Health

____

____

Mental and Educational

____

____

Spiritual

____

____

Social

____

____

Family and Home

____

____

Financial

____

____

Career

____

____

Exercise for Chapter 6: Change

This chart is similar to the one you filled out for Chapter 4: *The Seven Areas of Life*. This time, you'll be assessing the level of change in your life for the past six months:

5: Maximal change for the better
4: Intense change for the better
3: Considerable change for the better
2: Moderate change for the better
1: Mild change for the better
0: Neutral/can't tell
-1: Mild change for the worse
-2: Moderate change for the worse
-3: Considerable change for the worse
-4: Intense change for the worse
-5: Maximal change for the worse

Please score your current level of change in each area by putting a check mark in the appropriate box.

	-5	-4	-3	-2	-1	0	1	2	3	4	5
Physical and Health											
Mental and Educational											
Spiritual											
Social											
Family and Home											
Financial											
Career											

After filling out the C rows in the chart, please answer the following questions:

1. How has the level of change in my life over the past six months affected my overall level of happiness and satisfaction? *Why*?

2. How has change, positive or negative, been a source of grief in my life? How have I dealt with this grief?

3. How skillfully have I handled change over the past six months? What, if anything, can I do differently over the next six months?

Exercise for Chapter 7: Wellness

You have now taken a look at your Seven Areas of Life, rating for each your current level of pleasure and satisfaction and the amount of change you have experienced in the past six months. You've also learned a bit more about wellness. Now please look again at each of your Seven Areas of Life and write down how you could improve wellness in each. Keep in mind that improving wellness doesn't just mean eliminating pain and dissatisfaction. It can also mean improving pleasure and satisfaction.

My Ideas for Improving Wellness

Physical and Health

____

____

____

____

____

____

Mental and Educational

____

____

____

____

____

____

Spiritual

____

____

____

____

____

____

Social

Family and Home

Financial

Career

Exercise for Chapter 8: The Ladder of Fulfillment

Go through this worksheet as many times as necessary. You can also try going through it with your friends. It may introduce a new way of thinking that seems difficult at first, but the more you work with it, the easier it gets.

You probably will not use all the letters on this page. In fact, I usually do not have to climb further than five "rungs" with most clients. When you reach the goal that feels like your highest purpose, circle it and go on to the questions at the end of this exercise.

THE LADDER OF FULFILLMENT SELF-ASSESSMENT

What is a goal in your life that is important to you?

A. ______________________________

What would "A" do for you?

B. ______________________________

Which would you rather have—"A" or "B"? (Rewrite answer in following blank.)

C. ______________________________

What would "C" do for you?

D. ______________________________

Which would you rather have—"C" or "D"? (Rewrite answer in following blank.)

E. ______________________________

What would "E" do for you?

F. ______________________________

Which would you rather have—"E" or "F"? (Rewrite answer in following blank.)

G. ______________________________

What would "G" do for you?

H. ______________________________

Which would you rather have—"G" or "H"? (Rewrite answer in following blank.)

I. ____

What would "I" do for you? (Usually by this point what you have written seems to be an end in itself—in other words, your highest purpose or level of fulfillment.)

The following are questions to answer after you have circled your highest purpose or level of fulfillment. (If you have been unable to come up with an answer, don't worry. Continue reading this book and come back to this page when you are ready.)

1. Does the goal you have circled feel like your highest purpose or level of fulfillment? *Why* or *Why* not?

____

____

____

____

2. During the exercise, did you come up with any specific methods for finding your highest purpose? What are they?

____

____

____

____

3. What are some specific steps you can take today to move toward your highest purpose and attain fulfillment?

____

____

____

____

4. What are your feelings at this point about the exercise and what you have discovered? Do you feel closer to understanding your highest purpose and how to get there? *Why* or *Why* not?

____

____

____

____

GETTING TO *WHY*

Exercise for Chapter 9: The Three-Cylinder Engine of Personal Progress

Consider each of the cylinders of personal progress and assess how each is currently firing in your life. Also write down what you can do to improve each cylinder's performance.

My Three Cylinders of Personal Progress

Self-Motivation

Positive Attitude

Goal Direction

GETTING TO *WHY*

Exercise for Chapter 10: Self-Esteem

As we learned in the chapter, self-esteem often varies in each of our Seven Areas of Life. In this exercise, please assess and describe your level of self-esteem in each area and your overall self-esteem level. Are you a Self-Worshipper, Milquetoast, or Gutter Ball Champion? Is your self-esteem too low, too high, or just about right?

My Current Levels of Self-Esteem

Physical and Health

____

____

Mental and Educational

____

____

Spiritual

____

____

Social

____

____

Family and Home

____

____

Financial

____

____

Career

____

____

Exercise for Chapter 11: Saying 'No'

As we learned in the chapter, pursuing your highest purpose in life means saying "no" to many things in life that do not match that purpose. What are the top three things in your life you are having a hard time saying "no" to right now? In trying to think of what these might be, it may help to look at the Seven Areas of Life. People are often more assertive in one area than another. For example, a manager may be very good at saying no inside his or her company but have trouble doing the same at home.

1.

2.

3.

Exercise for Chapter 12: Fear and Doubt

As we discussed in the chapter, writing down your fears and doubts immediately reduces their power over you while increasing your power over them. Here you'll write down your Top 10 Fears. If you need to write more, use another sheet of paper. Don't stop until you get them all!

My Top 10 Fears

1. ______________________________

____

2. ______________________________

____

3. ______________________________

____

4. ______________________________

____

5. ______________________________

____

6. ______________________________

____

7. ______________________________

____

8. ______________________________

____

9. ______________________________

____

10. ______________________________

____

On the following pages is the Getting to ***Why*** Goal Planning Worksheet. The method for filling out the worksheet is detailed in the chapter. Your exercise is to practice filling out the worksheet for one goal in any of the Seven Areas of Life. If you get in a groove, try filling out the worksheet for a goal in a different area of life. Over the next week or so, try doing so for each of the seven areas. Of course, if you feel like filling out more than one worksheet for goals in the same area, please do so. It is incredibly empowering to have a stack of sheets and being able to say, "These are all of my goals."

GETTING TO *WHY*

Goal Planning Worksheet

Area of Life ______________________ **Today's Date** __________

Target Date ______________ **Achievement Date** ______________

Specific

My goal, stated as clearly and concretely as possible:

Measurable

I will use the following to measure progress and confirm achievement:

Attainable

I currently have/will acquire the following necessary abilities, skills, and qualifications:

Realistic

I have/will acquire the following necessary resources (time, money, etc.):

Trackable

I will do the following to track progress and confirm achievement:

Reality Check

For this goal to have meaning, I need to be able to answer "yes" to all three of these questions:

Does this goal support my values for this Area of Life? **YES / NO**
Does this goal help me get to *Why*? **YES / NO**
Is this goal worth the time, effort, and money it requires? **YES / NO**

Fear of Failure

My fears in detail, and what I'll do to overcome them:

Fear of Ridicule

Fear of Success

My Goal ______________________________

Benefits | Benefits to be gained (losses to be avoided) from achieving this goal:

Affirmations | Positive statements to boost my confidence and focus:

Action Steps Specific steps I will take to achieve my goal:	**Target Date**	**Review Date**	**Achievement Date**
1.			
2.			
3.			
4.			
5.			
6.			
7.			
8.			
9.			
10.			

Possible Obstacles	**Possible Solutions**
1.	**1.**
2.	**2.**
3.	**3.**
4.	**4.**
5.	**5.**

GETTING TO *WHY*

Exercise for Chapter 14: Self-Succession Planning

In the chapter, JB told his story about how a new ***Why*** came into his life, and he decided to become a minister. Most of us have gone through such a transformation in our lives, although we may not have fully understood what was happening to us at the time. Here, please describe a time when a new ***Why*** came into your life, including the people involved and how you processed the situation.

The Time a New *Why* Came into My Life

Exercise for Chapter 15: Your Personal Legacy

In the chapter, we talked about the importance of a personal legacy. Please write down your current vision for your personal legacy. This vision may very well change over time, but it's important to keep it in mind as you progress through life and get to ***Why***. Describe what you would like to leave behind in the world and how you'd like to change people's lives.

My Vision for My Personal Legacy

Exercise for Chapter 16: Synergy

1. What is an example of great synergy in my life from the past or present, and who was involved?

2. *Why* was the synergy so excellent in this instance?

3. In general, in what types of situations do I find myself experiencing great synergy with others?

Exercise for Chapter 17: Trust

Call to mind an important relationship in your life, present or past, in which you experienced or continue to experience a lack of trust. Identify the person and describe the problem. Then consider each of the three legs of the stool of trust and write down how the relationship was or is performing in that area. Finally, write down a possible solution to the problem. This is a useful exercise to go through anytime trust in a relationship is not what it should be.

A Relationship Requiring an Improvement of Trust

The Person ______________________________

The Problem

____

____

____

Leg 1: Communication

____

____

____

Leg 2: Understanding

____

____

____

Leg 3: Cooperation

____

____

____

Possible Solution

____

____

____

____

____

GETTING TO *WHY*

Exercise for Chapter 18: Direction

As we learned in the chapter, whether we are planning for the future or not, we all have a direction in life: the place where we will end up if we do not adjust our pitch and yaw. Please consider your current direction in each of the Seven Areas of Life and write it down. Then write down any adjustments that seem necessary at this time.

Physical and Health

Current Direction ______________________________

____

____

Adjustments to Be Made ______________________________

____

____

Mental and Educational

Current Direction ______________________________

____

____

Adjustments to Be Made ______________________________

____

____

Spiritual

Current Direction ______________________________

____

____

Adjustments to Be Made ______________________________

____

____

Social

Current Direction ______________________________

____

____

Social Continued...

Adjustments to Be Made ______________________________

____

____

Family and Home

Current Direction ______________________________

____

____

Adjustments to Be Made ______________________________

____

____

Financial

Current Direction ______________________________

____

____

Adjustments to Be Made ______________________________

____

____

Career

Current Direction ______________________________

____

____

Adjustments to Be Made ______________________________

____

____

Exercise for Chapter 19: The Manager's Role

As was stated in the chapter, the key to success as a manager is this: "Know your people." This rule applies in a company, church, family, or any organization. Choose an organization that's important to you and pick three people, describe what you don't know about them that you ought to know, and write down some steps you can take to improve the situation. This exercise may help you call to mind more people that you ought to know better. If so, keep writing and then take action!

People I Should Know Better

Organization ______________________________

Person 1 ______________________________

What I Don't Know ______________________________

____

____

Steps for Improvement ______________________________

____

____

Person 2 ______________________________

What I Don't Know ______________________________

____

____

Steps for Improvement ______________________________

____

____

Person 3 ______________________________

What I Don't Know ______________________________

____

____

Steps for Improvement ______________________________

____

____

Exercise for Chapter 20: The DAO Method

Consider a recent time that someone came to you with a question. The person could be subordinate, coworker, boss, friend, child, or anyone who was looking to you for an answer. Write down the question, and then consider how you would answer based on the DAO method of asking the questioner if he or she is looking for a decision, advice, or an opinion.

An Example of Using the DAO Method

Question I was asked

____

____

____

____

Making a decision

____

____

____

____

____

Providing advice

____

____

____

____

____

Providing an opinion

____

____

____

____

____

GETTING TO *WHY*

Exercise for Chapter 21: WIIFT? (What's In It For Them?)

Consider three people in your life with whom you'd like to improve the relationship. These people could be from work, church, your social sphere, your own family or anywhere else. Ask yourself, as concerns your relationship, "What's in it for them?" and what you could do to improve the relationship based on this. (Of course, if you are not certain, verifying what's in it for them later on could be very helpful. In the meantime, it's important to ask the question in order to get started.)

Person 1 ______________________________

Issues in the relationship ______________________________

____

What's in it for him/her in our relationship? ______________________________

____

Possible solution ______________________________

____

Person 2 ______________________________

Issues in the relationship ______________________________

____

What's in it for him/her in our relationship? ______________________________

____

Possible solution ______________________________

____

Person 3 ______________________________

Issues in the relationship ______________________________

____

What's in it for him/her in our relationship? ______________________________

____

Possible solution ______________________________

____

Worksheet and Exercise for Chapter 22: Delegation

On the following page is the Getting to ***Why*** Goal Delegation Planning Worksheet. The method for filling out the worksheet is detailed in the chapter. Your exercise is to practice filling out the worksheet for three tasks that you currently perform at your job, in your home, or in any area of life. The tasks can be ones you actually have the authority to delegate, or they can be tasks that you simply would like to delegate. Once you try filling out the sheet, you'll see just how easy and powerful it is as a tool.

Delegation Planning Worksheet

Note: The numbered steps correspond to the rights in the Delegatee's Bill of Rights.

Delegatee	**Delegator**	**Today's Date**

1A. Task	**1B. Deadline**

2A. Quality and Performance Expectations/Measurements

2B. Quality and Performance Tracking System

2C. Feedback Provider(s)	**2D. Feedback Date(s)**

3. Reason for Choosing Delegatee	**4A. Benefits to Delegatee**

4B. Benefits to Delegator

5. Task Priority and Delegation Level

	Delegatee's Tasks	Priority Rank (1 - 5)	Delegation Level (1 - 5)	6. Can This Task Be Delegated?	
1.	New Task			N/A	
2.				Yes	No
3.				Yes	No
4.				Yes	No
5.				Yes	No

7. Training and Tool Plan

	Training Step/Tool	Trainer	Target Date	Date Completed/ Provided
1.				
2.				
3.				
4.				
5.				

Delegation Planning Worksheet Reference Sheet

The Levels of Delegation

1. Don't do anything until I tell you.

2. Check with me before you do it. Report back right after you do it.

3. Check with me before you do it. Report back routinely (daily, weekly, monthly).

4. Do it. Report back right after you do it.

5. Do it. Report back routinely (daily, weekly, monthly).

The Delegatee's Bill of Rights

For every task delegated, a delgatee has the right to know and provide his or her opinion on the following:

1. What the task and deadline are.

2. What level of task quality and performance is expected, how quality and performance will be measured and tracked, and how and when feedback will be provided.

3. Why the task is being delegated to him or her and not someone else.

4. What the benefits of delegation are for both the delegator and the delegatee.

5. How the task ranks in priority compared to other tasks for which the delegatee is responsible.

6. Whether one or more of the delegatee's current tasks can be delegated to others so that the delegatee can focus on the new task.

7. Who is going to train or coach the delegatee and what are the steps of that training. What are the tools needed (computer, production equipment, or anything needed to perform the task), and who will provide the training on them.

Delegator ______________________ **Delegatee** ______________________

Date ______________________ **Date** ______________________

GETTING TO *WHY*

Exercise for Chapter 23: Succession Planning

Succession planning may be necessary in any organization in which you play a role, including work, religious organization, clubs, and family, to name just a few. Write down an organization in which you participate, your role, and five steps you need to take in order to realize succession in each. For example, every parent should have a will, and every worker should have a job description (even if the boss has not provided one). If performing this exercise motivates you to fill out relevant Goal Planning Worksheets or Delegation Planning Worksheets, all the better. Keep in mind that it's crucial to have a succession plan in place, even if you don't believe the plan will be necessary for years to come.

Organization ______________________________

My Role ______________________________

____

____

____

Step for succession 1 ______________________________

____

____

Step for succession 2 ______________________________

____

____

Step for succession 3 ______________________________

____

____

Step for succession 4 ______________________________

____

____

Step for succession 5 ______________________________

____

____

Made in the USA
Lexington, KY
08 June 2017